1500+ DAYS OF RECIPES

HEART HEALTHY
COOKBOOK

TRANSFORM YOUR HEART HEALTH
WITH 1500+ DAYS OF LOW-SODIUM,
LOW-FAT RECIPES

Copyright Notice:
© Grace Garner. All rights reserved. No part of this book may be reproduced, distributed, or transmitted in any form or by any means, without the prior written permission of the author or the publisher, except in the case of brief quotations embodied in critical reviews and certain other noncommercial uses permitted by copyright law. For permission requests, write to the publisher, addressed "Attention: Permissions Coordinator," at [your email or physical address].

Liability Disclaimer:
The publisher and author have made every effort to ensure the accuracy and completeness of the information contained in this book. However, neither the publisher nor the author assumes any responsibility for errors, omissions, or contrary interpretation of the subject matter herein. This book is presented "as is" without express or implied warranties. Neither the publisher nor the author shall be liable for any physical, psychological, emotional, financial, or commercial damages, prosecutions, or proceedings incurred as a result of the information provided in this book.

Usage Disclaimer:
This book is intended for informational and entertainment purposes only. The views expressed herein are the personal opinions of the author, and the information provided does not constitute legal, medical, financial or professional advice. Readers are advised to seek appropriate professional consultation before acting upon any information contained in this book.

By reading this book, you acknowledge and agree that you assume the risks associated with any actions you take based on the content of this book and release the author and publisher from any liability.

Acknowledgment of Understanding:
By proceeding beyond this page, the reader acknowledges and agrees to all the terms and conditions set forth within this disclaimer and affirms an understanding of the same.

Severability:
If any provision of this disclaimer is found to be unenforceable, the remaining provisions will continue in full force and effect.

ISBN 979-8-86-222112-1

TABLE OF CONTENTS

❈ HERE ARE YOUR FREE GIFTS!
☟ SCAN HERE TO DOWNLOAD IT

SCAN HERE

8-Week Meal Plan Grocery List: Kickstart your heart-healthy journey with a ready-made grocery list tailored for our 8-week meal plan. No guesswork, just grab and go!

Master Grocery List: A template featuring the most common heart-healthy foods. Quickly jot down what you need for your recipes and take it shopping—effortless and efficient.

Blank Recipe Card: Discover a new favorite? Note it down and make it a heart-healthy classic in your kitchen.

Foods to Eat & Avoid Cards: A quick cheat sheet to keep your meals heart friendly. Know what to embrace and what to avoid at a glance.

Weekly Meal Plan Template: Flex your culinary creativity with a template to plan your own heart-healthy week. Your taste buds—and your heart—will thank you.

Introduction

In an era where busy and hectic schedules, temptations for fast food, and inactive lifestyles have become the new norm, the statistics regarding heart issues are nothing short of alarming. But let's not dive solely into the grim realities and daunting numbers. Instead, I want to talk about what hope is there for us and what we can do to avert the risks of cardiac diseases. It's time to address all the underlying factors responsible for causing heart disease and look towards a powerful solution that lies right in your kitchen—the heart-healthy diet.

If you are looking for a means to optimize your heart health through diet and lifestyle changes, then this cookbook has all the right answers. It is your ultimate key to unlocking a world full of luscious, heart-healthy meals that will not only provide nourishment but also a variety of flavors for your taste buds.

With my mantra of 'Flavor-First, Health Always,' I believe that managing health conditions like cardiac disease, diabetes, or renal issues should never mean compromising on the good flavors and the joy of eating. So, keeping that core belief in mind, I have crafted this cookbook. This is why this is more than just a collection of recipes; it is a lifestyle guide for those looking to make health-conscious choices without compromising on taste. It has 150+ meticulously created recipes, each designed to satisfy your palate and to create heart-healthy meals for over 1500+ days. The brilliance lies in the variety: with these recipes, you have the freedom to create endless combinations that keep your diet diverse. This ensures your journey toward heart health is full of flavor and sustainability.

Through the text of this cookbook, you will learn about the fantastic impact of whole foods, the importance of cutting down sodium and unhealthy fats from your diet, and the transformative advantages of regular physical exercise. It is really going to help you transform your diet and lifestyle;

you just need to start picking up the right recipes and make better dietary decisions from now on!

Now, let's explore the content of this cookbook, try all the heart-friendly recipes, and follow the meal plans. Experience the power of a heart-healthy diet yourself. Your heart is your most valuable possession—let's celebrate it, nurture it, and make sure it beats strong for years to come.

Understanding Heart Health

The importance of heart health cannot be over-emphasized when it comes to longevity and aging. A healthy heart is crucial for longer and more fulfilling life. With age the risk of developing cardiovascular diseases increases significantly. By prioritizing heart health, you can reduce the likelihood of encountering these diseases, allowing yourself to enjoy a higher quality of life well into your later years. Maintaining a healthy heart through regular exercise, a balanced diet, and managing health risks like high blood pressure or hypertension, high cholesterol, and diabetes can significantly decrease the chances of heart-related complications. Moreover, a healthy heart promotes overall well-being, enabling individuals to remain active, independent, and engaged in their daily lives as they age. By nurturing heart health, you can not only extend their lifespan but also enhance their ability to enjoy their golden years with vitality and vigor.

The Role of Diet in Heart Health

Whatever we eat plays a vital role in maintaining the health of our hearts and preventing cardiovascular diseases. Any diet loaded with whole foods, like vegetables, fruits, whole grains, lean proteins, and healthy fats, is going to do wonders for our body and its organs, especially the heart. These foods offer essential nutrients, antioxidants, and fiber that keep the cardiac muscles strong and pumping. They help keep the blood cholesterol levels maintained while naturally managing the blood pressure and reducing inflammation, which we know are the major risk factors for heart disease. Through a diet, we can limit the intake of saturated as well as trans fats, cholesterol, sodium, and added sugars, which are the major contributors to the development of cardiovascular problems. So, by adopting a balanced and nutritious diet, you can alleviate the risk of heart disease, strengthen your blood vessels, maintain a healthy weight, and support overall cardiovascular well-being.

The Heart Healthy Diet

The term heart-healthy diet was coined for all the dietary approaches that recommend eating food that doesn't contain any saturated fats, lots of sugar, or processed food items. You see, high-caloric food with lots of saturated fats can raise the number of Low-density lipoproteins -bad cholesterol in the blood vessels of a person, and the accumulation of such bad cholesterol can increase the risk of cardiac problems, including narrowing of blood cardiac vessels or in some cases stroke due to blockage of vessels. The heart-healthy diet offers a simple solution to this problem; it recommends eating food with low levels of bad cholesterol, saturated fats, and refined carbs. Instead, it suggests the intake of healthy fats, proteins, complex carbs, and lots of fiber, minerals, and vitamins, along with water.

Nutritional Needs for Heart Health

When it comes to heart health, consuming a perfect mix of healthy nutrients is most important. For instance, if you start consuming lots of bad cholesterol and refined carbohydrates, then your body will suffer from obesity, high blood pressure, or high blood cholesterol levels. So, consume those nutrients that are best at meeting the nutritional requirements of your heart, such as:

Healthy Fats: Adding healthy source of fats into your daily diet is crucial. Such fats include monounsaturated fats that are present in olive oil, avocados, and nuts, as well as polyunsaturated fats found in flaxseeds, fatty fish, walnuts, and chia seeds. These fats play a central role in alleviating the levels of bad or LDL cholesterol in the blood and countering the risk of heart disease.

Omega-3 Fatty Acids: They contain polyunsaturated fats. These healthy fats are most dominantly found in fatty fish, flaxseeds, walnuts, and chia seeds. Omega-3s contribute to reducing unhealthy triglyceride levels, calming down inflammation, and aiding optimal heart and blood vessel function.

Fiber: It is essential to have a diet abundant in dietary fiber, especially soluble fiber, to reduce cholesterol levels in the blood and manage a healthy weight. When you incorporate a good number of legumes, fruits, whole grains, nuts, vegetables, and seeds into your diet, it guarantees a sufficient intake of fiber.

Antioxidants: Antioxidants work against the health-harming radicals and toxins present in our bodies. They are found in juicy and colorful fruits and vegetables, and they play a vital role in countering oxidative stress and inflammation, both of which are known risk factors for heart disease.

Potassium: Speaking of maintaining healthy blood pressure levels, it also calls for an adequate intake of potassium. To achieve that, eat more potassium-rich foods, for instance, bananas, oranges, spinach, sweet potatoes, and beans.

Magnesium: It plays a vital role in regulating normal heart beat and blood pressure. You can source a good amount of magnesium by adding sources like leafy greens, nuts, whole grains, seeds, and legumes to your diet.

Calcium and Vitamin D: They help support the function of the heart muscles. Calcium is necessary for muscles and bones, whereas vitamin D aids in the absorption of calcium in the body. For a heart-healthy diet, you can source both those nutrients from low-fat dairy products, leafy greens, and fatty fish.

Sodium: It is a known fact that high consumption of sodium can increase our blood pressure, which in turn elevates the risk of heart disease. To cut your sodium intake, I would like to advise you to avoid table salt and go for low-sodium alternatives whenever possible. It is worth mentioning here that most excessed and packaged foods contain high amounts of sodium; thus, it is important to carefully read food labels and avoid the pros that contain too much sodium. It is best to keep the sodium to 2000-2500mg/ day to keep your blood pressure maintained.

B Vitamins: When we consume vitamin B complex, which includes vitamin B6, vitamin B12, and folate, through our diet, it can help reduce the levels of homocysteine, a type of amino acid linked to an increased risk of heart disease. To make sure that you can have an adequate amount of these vitamins in your diet, try to include food items like leafy greens, legumes, lean meats, poultry, fortified cereals, fish, and eggs in your dietary choices.

Limit Added Sugars and Trans Fats: The risk of heart disease gets amplified by the consumption of refined carbs, added sugars, and trans fats. To avoid such a risk, it is imperative to reduce the intake of sugary drinks, sweets, deep-fried snacks, and foods that may have partially hydrogenated oils in them.

Foods to Enjoy and Foods to Avoid

The heart-healthy diet is a two-pronged approach that not only limits the intake of sodium, sugary items, saturated fats, or unhealthy food products, but it also recommends you incorporate more of the healthy food rich in fibers and vitamins into your daily diet, such as:

Veggies and fruits: Adding a wide range of colorful fruits and vegetables to the diet is highly beneficial as they are rich in fiber, antioxidants, vitamins, and minerals. The best way to incorporate more veggies and fruits into your diet is to have a variety of salads and smoothies on your menu.

Whole Grains: Instead of relying on processed or refined carbs, go for whole grain options which have high fiber content:

- Whole wheat bread
- Brown rice
- Quinoa
- Oats
- Whole grain pasta

Seafood: Fish loaded with omega 3s are a healthy source of proteins and healthy fat. You can add options like salmon, mackerel, trout, and sardines to your meals, as they are a great source of omegas that have been proven to decrease the risk of heart disease.

Legumes: Another fat-free source of proteins you can rely on is legumes. You can add beans, lentils, and chickpeas, which are loaded with fibers, proteins, and other nutrients that promote heart health.

Seeds and Nuts: Add a variety of nuts and seeds to your meals, like walnuts, almonds, flaxseeds, chia seeds, and pumpkin seeds, as they are a rich and healthy source of fats, fiber, and antioxidants.

Healthy Fats: Fats found in avocado, olive, and canola oil are all healthy and must be incorporated into this diet. These fats offer only good cholesterol, which is great for heart health.

Low-fat dairy: Yes, you can eat dairy on this diet, but since full-fat dairy products contain saturated fats, it is recommended to consume low-fat dairy products. Alternatively, you can also try plant-based dairy alternatives, like fortified soy milk or almond milk, which are low in saturated fat.

Foods to Limit or Avoid:

The aim of the heart-healthy diet is to keep the body from nutrients that would raise the blood pressure, clog the arteries, or weaken the heart muscles. So, keeping that goal in mind, here is what you should avoid or limit on your diet:

Fatty meat cut:

All the meat cuts which contain visible fats are not suitable to consume on this diet. Those meat cuts include:

- Ribeye steak: This popular meat cut is recognized for its marble-like look, which is because of the appearance of fat content throughout the meat, making it tender and flavorful but highly dangerous for health.
- Pork belly: Again, this cut is also heavily marbled with fat, which gives it a juicy and succulent taste but is highly unhealthy.
- Lamb shoulder: It has a relatively higher fat content. If you are using lamb meat for a recipe, make sure to avoid this cut.

Full-fat dairy products:

All full-fat dairy products contain a higher percentage of saturated fat. Some full-fat dairy products that you need to avoid are:

- Whole milk: It contains around 3.5% fat, which makes it creamy and rich.
- Full-fat yogurt: This one is made from whole milk, and it has a higher fat content.
- Cheese: Cheeses like cheddar, gouda, and brie are loaded with fat. So, while you are buying cheeses for your menu, make sure to buy the low-fat versions of those cheeses.

Butter:

Its high fat content makes it not suitable for this diet. Some widely available types of butter that you need to watch out for include:

- Salted butter
- Unsalted butter

High-fat processed foods:

All such food items, such as deep-fried food, contain high sodium content, preservatives, fats, and oils. Some examples include:

- Potato chips: They are often cooked in unhealthy oils and can be high in fats. It is best to incorporate homemade chips baked in the oven or air fryer to reduce the oil content.
- Pastries and cakes: The baked goods that we buy from stores, like croissants, doughnuts, and cakes, often contain preservatives, saturated fats, butter, and saturated oils.
- Processed meats: Meats like hot dogs, sausages, and bacon contain high amounts of fats, so they must be avoided.

Trans fats:

These fats are formed when liquid oils are processed into solid fats. These fats are highly dangerous for the cardiovascular system. They are widely found in processed and fried foods. Examples of trans-fat sources include:

- Margarine
- Deep-fried foods cooked in trans-oils

Fried food:

Any food that is deep fried in oil or fat is not a suitable fit for this diet. To keep the diet healthy, try the oil-free homemade versions of these food items. Examples include:

- French fries.
- Fried chicken
- Spring rolls

While cutting down the intake of the above-mentioned products, make sure to reduce your intake of sugars and sugar-carrying drinks, desserts, candies, and processed snacks.

Besides that, also control your sodium intake by using less salt and avoiding high-sodium food products like canned soups, sauces, and processed meats.

Lastly, limit your alcohol intake to moderate amounts. And control the consumption of high-cholesterol foods, like shellfish, organ meats, and egg yolks.

Seasonal Produce Guide

Instead of relying on processed or frozen vegetables and fruits, it is better to make use of the fresh seasonal fruits and veggies that are readily available. Seasonal produce is available in fresh and organic form at a very reasonable price. Some of the seasonal fruits and veggies that you can use in each season include:

Spring:

- Leafy greens: Kale, Swiss chard, spinach, and arugula are leafy vegetables that are loaded with vitamins, minerals, and antioxidants.
- Berries: All types of berries, from blueberries to strawberries, cranberries, etc., are easily available in this season, and they are packed with antioxidants and fiber.
- Asparagus: It is a nutrient-dense vegetable you can find in spring, and It is a good source of folate and fiber.
- Radishes: These juicy and crunchy veggies make a great addition to the salads, and they are low in calories and high in fiber and vitamin C.
- Peas: Freshly harvested peas are a good source of vitamins, fiber, and minerals. You can use them in salads, rice, and curries.

Summer:

- Tomatoes: In summer, you can find all varieties of tomatoes with ease. They are juicy, vibrant, and loaded with lycopene-which is an antioxidant good for heart.
- Watermelon: Highly hydrating and refreshing, it has lower caloric content and higher amount of vitamins A and C.
- Bell peppers: They are colorful, crisp, and loaded with antioxidants and vitamin C.
- Zucchini: A versatile summer squash that is low in calories and high in fiber.

- Corn: Enjoy fresh corn on the cob, which provides various vitamins and minerals.

Fall:

- Apples: They are crunchy and full of fiber.
- Pears: Juicy and sweet, they are a good source of fiber and vitamin C.
- Brussels sprouts: Also known as mini cabbages, Brussels sprouts are loaded with fiber, vitamins, and minerals.
- Squash: There are a lot of different varieties of acorn squash, butternut squash, and pumpkin, and they all are packed with antioxidants and provide fiber.
- Cauliflower: It is a great vegetable that can be used in a variety of recipes. If you want to lose some weight or control your caloric intake, then cauliflower is a great option to try.

Winter:

- Citrus fruits: In winter, you can enjoy the goodness of oranges, grapefruits, and clementines. These citrus fruits are loaded with vitamin C and antioxidants.
- Kiwi: it is a small, refreshing fruit that is stuffed with fiber, vitamin C, and antioxidants.
- Root vegetables: Veggies that grow underground, like carrots, beets, turnips, and parsnips, are all nutrient-dense, and they provide fiber and various vitamins.
- Cabbage: Loaded with fiber, cabbage is a cruciferous veggie that provides heart-protective benefits.
- Winter greens: From collard greens to kale and Swiss chard, all leafy greens can be enjoyed in hearty soups and stews.

AHA Lifestyle Recommendations

The American Heart Association-AHA is a nonprofit organization in the United States that is dedicated to fighting cardiovascular diseases and stroke. Besides a healthy diet, AHA also suggests that adults must aim for a minimum of 150 minutes of moderate-level aerobic activity or at least 75 minutes of intense aerobic activity every week. For instance, you can do cycling, swimming, brisk walking, or dancing. To maximize the benefits, it is advised to spread out physical activity and strive for at least 30 minutes or more moderate-level aerobic activity daily or thrive twice a week.

AHA also recommends practicing moderation when it comes to consuming alcohol. It suggests 2 standard drinks a day per person for men and up to 1 drink a day per person for women. A standard drink contains 14 grams of alcohol, equivalent to approximately 5 ounces of wine, 12 ounces of beer, or 1.5 ounces of distilled spirits. It is essential to be mindful of the calorie content in alcoholic beverages, as they can contribute to weight gain and potential health issues.

To effectively incorporate a heart-healthy diet into your lifestyle, AHA also recommends making your friends and family part of this journey. You can plan the diet plan and explore new healthy recipes with your family, and together, you can improve the overall health of everyone in the house. With friends, you can make sure to eat at restaurants and places where they serve more heart-healthy meals. Such tactics really make it easier for a person to harness the benefits of a heart-healthy lifestyle.

Practical Tips for a Heart-Healthy Diet

Sticking to a heart-healthy dietary approach with consistency is not easy; it is a road where you may get distracted by tons of unhealthy options. Yes, you will face various challenges along the way. With tons of processed food products available in our fast-paced society, it is difficult to follow one consistent path. Time constraints, busy schedules, and limited cooking abilities can also make it challenging to consistently prepare nourishing meals at home. Nevertheless, there are strategies to counter those challenges. And in this chapter, I

am going to discuss all the practical ways to overcome any problem that would come your way:

Grocery Shopping Tips

If you go grocery shopping on an empty stomach, the chances are that you will end up buying lots of sugary food and beverages. That's what our mind does when it doesn't get enough glucose- it makes you buy things out of impulse. But you can take some precautionary measures to stop that from happening. If you want to follow a healthy diet, then make sure to lay out a plan before going out on your grocery store trips.

Jot Down the list: You cannot buy random stuff from the aisle. What goes in your cart must be according to your meal plan. So, create a list of ingredients according to your menu and then follow that list. Having a categorized list will keep you focused, and it will reduce the chances of impulse buying.

Shop the perimeter: The aisles at the perimeter of the grocery store mostly contain fresh seasonal produce, lean proteins, and dairy products, so make sure to visit those aisles first and stuff your cart with more of those products.

Try more fresh produce: The more you stock up on a colorful variety of fresh fruits and vegetables, the better. These nutrient-dense products have fewer calories and an adequate amount of fiber, vitamins, minerals, and antioxidants in them. Your goal should be a diverse selection, including seasonal veggies, citrus fruits, berries, leafy greens, and cruciferous vegetables.

Choose whole grains: In the grains and legumes section, try to pick up whole grains instead of refined ones. Whole wheat, quinoa, brown rice, oats, etc., are some of the best options.

Pick lean proteins: In the meat section, search for lean and low-fat meat like poultry, fish, legumes, and tofu. If you want to buy red meat, then choose leaner cuts of meat and then remove their visible fats before cooking. Do not buy processed meats like hot dogs, sausages, and deli meats, as they are rich in sodium and unhealthy fats.

Read food labels: Develop this habit of reading the food labels of the food products you are buying. Reading the labels gives you a clear idea of whether the product is suitable to take home or not.

Be cautious of marketing claims: Many edible products come with claims like "low fat" or "reduced sugar." But not all of them are true. It's imperative to read the entire label carefully and evaluate the nutritional profile of the food before bringing it home.

Shop on a full stomach: Never buy anything from the grocery shop when you are hungry, as it makes you buy things impulsively.

Choose water or unsweetened beverages: Staying hydrated is important, so make sure to add water or unsweetened drinks like herbal tea or infused water to your cart instead of sugary beverages or sodas.

Reading Food Labels

Food labels are printed on the food products to offer you valuable information about the contents of the products. They offer important information about the nutritional content of packaged foods, which helps us to make better choices and manage our cardiovascular health. By carefully reading the labels, we can learn about the presence of heart-healthy nutrients while being cautious about harmful components like trans fats, saturated fats, sodium, and added sugars. Here is how you must read labels before buying the food products:

Consider the serving size: Start by checking the serving size present on the label. This information is essential because all the nutrient values are provided according to this serving size. Make sure to compare it with the portion size you typically consume.

Pay attention to total calories: Look at the calorie count per serving. This will give you a good idea of the energy levels of the food. If you are keeping an eye on your calorie intake, be mindful of the number of calories per serving.

Evaluate fat content: Assess the total fat content and the breakdown of the fat content into saturated fat and trans fat. Try foods that are low in saturated as well as trans fats.

Look for fiber and whole grains: Sufficient fiber intake is highly beneficial for heart health. So, look into the fiber content on the label and select foods that are loaded with fibers.

Watch for added sugars: Sugars contribute to excessive calorie intake and can increase the risk of obesity and cardiac disease. Scan the ingredient list of each product and different sources of added sugars like corn syrup, dextrose, or sucrose, then make your decision.

Assess nutrient percentages: The "% Daily Value" (%DV) present on food labels shows how much of a specific nutrient is present in one serving compared to the recommended daily intake. Make sure to choose foods that have lower levels of saturated fat, cholesterol, trans fat, and sodium while being rich in fiber, vitamins, and minerals.

Kitchen Tools and Equipment

With all the right tools in the kitchen, you can cook all sorts of flavorsome meals at home without spending extra time and effort in the kitchen. In simple words, they make the job easy for you. Some of the essential tools that I would like to recommend here include:

- **Chef's knife**: A well-honed and sharp chef's knife is a great instrument. Consider getting a top-notch knife that provides a good grip and fine cutting.
- **Cutting board**: A quality cutting board is an basic tool for preparing ingredients. Look out for a cutting board created from

bamboo, plastic, or wood, as they are easy to clean and gentle for the knife's edge.

- **Non-stick pans**: Such pans and pots are easy to clean, and they require less oil or cooking spray for cooking, making them suitable for an oil-free diet. Select high-quality, non-toxic pans with a durable, non-stick surface.
- **Baking sheet:** It is handy for baking or roasting veggies, chicken or fish, and healthy snacks like roasted chickpeas. Look for a quality baking sheet that heats evenly.
- **Steamer basket**: Steaming is a great cooking method that allows you to cook oil-free, healthy meals. That is why it is probably a good idea to have a steamer basket or a steamer insert for your pot to steam all sorts of vegetables, fish, or other ingredients.
- **Blender or food processor:** From creating smoothies, homemade sauces, dips, and dressings, a blender or processor can really make your life easy.
- **Salad spinner**: It makes it easy to wash and dry veggies, especially leafy greens, which are widely used in a heart-healthy diet.
- **Measuring cups and spoons:** Precise measurement is important for maintaining portion control. So, have a set of calibrated cups and spoons on hand for correct measurements of ingredients.
- **Food storage containers**: Having a wide variety of food storage containers in different sizes makes it easy to store leftovers. Go for BPA-free, microwave-safe, and airtight containers.
- **Immersion blender:** It is my go-to kitchen companion. Also known as a hand blender, it is great at pureeing soups, sauces, and smoothies directly in the container.
- **Spiralizer**: If you love to make vegetable noodles from zucchini, carrots, or other firm vegetables, then spiralize is the perfect tool for that.
- **Grater/zester:** A grater or zester is highly useful for adding zesty flavors of citrus zest, grated ginger, or shredded cheese. It's also good for grating vegetables like carrots or zucchini for salads or stir-fries.

Embracing Flavors

Eating healthy food doesn't have to be boring. There are several amazing ways in which you can add a variety of flavors to your meals and make them tempting and delicious while using all the healthy ingredients. Even on a heart-healthy diet, you can use the following ways to create delicious meals at home:

Good use of herbs and spices: Herbs and spices are the best flavor enhancers that can transform a meal. Explore a wide range of herbs like basil, cilantro, rosemary, and thyme, as well as spices like cumin, paprika, turmeric, and cinnamon. These ingredients can infuse your meals with richness and intricacy, improving their flavor profile without the need for salt or unhealthy fats.

Add citrus zest and juice: Sprinkle a little citrus zest or a squeeze of lemon, lime, or orange juice over food can spike up the flavors of your dishes. They add a refreshing tanginess that complements salads, steamed or roasted vegetables, and grilled meats.

Add aromatics like garlic and onions: These aromatics bring rich, savory flavors to your meals. Sautéing garlic and onions in a small amount of heart-healthy oil can add depth of flavors to a wide range of dishes.

Use a variety of cooking methods: When we use different cooking methods like grilling, baking, roasting, and steaming, we get to enhance the natural flavors of the food.

Experiment with vinegar: Vinegar can add a richness of flavors to a variety of meals. Some types of vinegar, like balsamic, apple cider, and red wine vinegar, can add a tangy and mildly sweet flavor to salads, marinades, and sauces.

Try some umami-rich ingredients: Umami is the fifth taste sensation known for its savory, satisfying flavor. Foods like mushrooms, tomatoes, soy sauce, miso paste, and nutritional yeast are all rich in umami and can enhance the taste of your dishes.

Choose high-quality ingredients: Fresh, seasonal, and high-quality ingredients often have more intense flavors. Opt for ripe, juicy fruits, vibrant vegetables, and flavorful herbs to make your dishes more delicious.

Always use healthy fats: While it's important to consume healthy fats in moderation, using small amounts of heart-healthy oils like olive oil, avocado oil, or nut oils can add a luxurious mouthfeel and depth of flavor to your dishes.

Portion Control

Portion control simply means that you will create a balance of ingredients and nutrients in every meal you eat. It helps in regulating calorie intake, managing weight, and avoiding excessive consumption. For instance, according to the nutritional profile, here is how you can manage the portion of your meals:

Protein:

- Lean meats (chicken, turkey, fish): A serving size is about 3-4 ounces, which is almost the size of the palm of your hand.
- Beans and legumes: A serving size is about ½ cup, or the size of a tennis ball.
- Tofu or tempeh: A serving size is about 3-4 ounces, similar to lean meats.
- Nuts and seeds: A serving size is about 1 ounce, equivalent to a small handful.

Grains:

- Cooked rice, quinoa, or pasta: A serving size is about ½ cup or the size of a hockey puck.
- Whole grain bread: A serving size is typically one slice.

- Whole grain cereals: A serving size is typically ¾ to 1 cup.
- Fruits: A serving size is typically one medium-sized fruit (e.g., apple, orange) or ½ cup of chopped fruits.
- Vegetables: A serving size is about ½ cup of cooked vegetables or 1 cup of raw leafy greens.

Dairy:

- Milk or yogurt: A serving size is about 1 cup.
- Cheese: A serving size is typically 1-1.5 oz., which is about the size of your thumb.
- Fats and oils:
- Cooking oils: A serving size is about one teaspoon or the size of a thumb tip.
- Nut butter: A serving size is typically two tablespoons.
- Salad dressings: A serving size is about two tablespoons.

Tips for Dining Out and Social Events

When you are following a certain dietary approach, it gets difficult to eat out without compromising on the dietary standards. More often than usual, people stop socializing or eating out with friends just because of this reason, or sometimes, people end up compromising their diets at social events. Well, I have a middle way for you! By being mindful and careful of your dietary options to manage your diet at social events or restaurants. Let me tell you how:

Research and choose restaurants wisely: Search for restaurants that offer heart-healthy options or have menus with a variety of nutritious choices. Several restaurants now publish nutritional information online, which can help you make informed selections ahead of time.

Plan in Advance: If you know you will be dining out, start planning your meals ahead of time. Eat lighter, nutrient-dense meals before dining out to balance out any potential indulgences later on.

Practice portion control: At most restaurants, portions served are usually greater than the portion size we consume. So, instead of eating it all, control your portion size and consider sharing an entrée with a friend or ask the staff to pack the leftovers.

Meal Menu:

There will be a lot of items on the menu that you cannot consume on your diet, so you can always look for healthier alternatives for those ingredients, such as

- Instead of fried or breaded meals, ask for baked, grilled, or steamed options.
- Order lean protein sources such as grilled chicken, fish, or legumes.
- Focus more on your vegetable intake by choosing salads, vegetable-based sides, or steamed options.
- Ask for dressings, sauces, and curries on the side to have control over the amount you consume.

Be cautious with beverages: Drinks served at restaurants, including sodas, sweetened iced teas, and alcoholic beverages, all contain lots of carbs and empty calories, which can negatively impact heart health. So, it is best to order water or unsweetened tea.

Socialize away from the food table: At social events, do not engage in conversation and activities near the buffet or snack table, as you might end up eating something unhealthy. Socialize away from the food table to reduce mindless snacking and grazing.

Bring a heart-healthy dish: If you are attending a social gathering, you can consider bringing a heart-healthy dish that you enjoy. This makes sure that you have a nutritious option to enjoy.

Communicate your dietary preferences: Don't hesitate to communicate your dietary limitations to the host. They may be able to accommodate your dietary needs or provide alternative options.

Adapting Heart Healthy Diet for Special Conditions

The same heart-healthy diet can be adjusted to meet the needs of specific healthy conditions to promote optimal health outcomes. Let's explore the different ways in which we can incorporate and customize a heart-healthy diet for each of these conditions:

Diabetes:

If you have diabetes, you must prioritize blood sugar management while adopting a heart-healthy diet. Managing diabetes and maintaining heart health are closely linked; as someone with diabetes, you are at a greater risk of developing cardiac disease. You can adjust the heart-healthy diet to make it appropriate for diabetes management. It's imperative to focus on nutritious foods that help control blood sugar levels and promote cardiovascular health. Here are some guidelines to consider:

Control portion sizes: Look out your portion sizes to manage calorie intake and maintain a healthy weight. This is essential for managing diabetes and reducing the risk of heart disease.

Choose complex carbohydrates: It is best to go for whole grains like brown rice, whole grains bread, and quinoa instead of refined carbs. These complex carbohydrates have a lesser impact on blood sugar levels and provide more fiber, vitamins, and minerals.

Include plenty of non-starchy vegetables: Eat more of the non-starchy vegetables like leafy greens, broccoli, peppers, tomatoes, and carrots. These are low in calories, rich in fiber, and high in essential nutrients.

Choose low-glycemic index foods: Add foods with a low glycemic index (GI) to your diet. These foods gradually increase the blood sugar levels. Some low-GI foods include whole grains, legumes, nuts, and vegetables.

Monitor carbohydrate intake: Keep track of your carbs and sugar intake and distribute the total intake evenly throughout the day to manage blood sugar levels.

High Blood Pressure:

For people with high blood pressure and hypertension, modifying a heart-healthy diet calls for a crucial reduction in sodium intake. The goal is to consume 2,300 mg of sodium/ day or even less. Avoid processed or packaged foods, as they are often loaded with sodium.

Increase potassium intake: Potassium helps counteract the effects of sodium on blood pressure. So add potassium-rich foods to your diet, like oranges, bananas, leafy greens, potatoes, tomatoes, avocados, and beans.

Choose whole grains: when you consume whole grains like whole wheat bread, brown rice, quinoa, and oats, they provide more fiber and nutrients compared to refined grains, which promotes heart health and helps manage blood pressure.

Increase fiber intake: Consuming sufficient fiber can help control blood pressure levels. The heart-healthy diet already recommends whole food, which contains a good amount of fiber, so as long as you are sticking to the heart-healthy diet, your fiber consumption is good to go. Just make sure to consume at least 25-30 grams of fiber per day.

Weight Loss:

While following a heart-healthy diet with weight loss objectives, the primary goal is to achieve a calorie deficit and meet all the basic nutritional requirements.

Create a calorie deficit: The very standard method of losing weight is to burn more calories than your body consumes. Or have fewer calories than you can burn. So, when you limit your calorie intake, you create a calorie deficit, which in turn helps you lose weight. Calculate your daily calorie needs depending on your age, gender, amount of activity, and weight loss goals. Try to go for a moderate calorie deficit of around 500-750 calories per day to achieve gradual and sustainable weight loss.

Prioritize whole, unprocessed foods: Select whole grains, fruits, vegetables, lean proteins, and healthy fats as the foundation of your diet. These foods are nutrient-dense and support heart health.

Portion control: Pay attention to serving sizes to manage average calorie intake. Use measuring cups, a food scale, or visual cues to control each portion. Be mindful of high-calorie foods, even if they are heart-healthy, as consuming them in excess can obstruct the process of weight loss.

Focus on fruits and vegetables: Stuff your plate with a wide variety of colorful fruits and vegetables. They are low in calories, high in fiber, and rich in essential vitamins and minerals. They help you feel full while providing important nutrients for heart health.

Choose lean proteins: Go for lean protein sources like poultry, fish, legumes, tofu, and low-fat dairy products. Protein helps achieve satiety and preserve muscle mass during weight loss.

Include healthy fats: Add sources of healthy fats like avocados, nuts, seeds, and olive oil. Healthy fats provide satiety and contribute to heart health. However, be mindful of serving sizes as fats are calorie-dense.

Minimize processed and sugary foods: Limit or avoid processed and sugary foods like sugary beverages, packaged snacks, sweets, and processed meats. These foods are often rich in calories, unhealthy fats, sodium, and added sugars, which can prevent weight loss.

Plan meals and snacks: Plan your meals and snacks ahead of time to avoid making impulsive and unhealthy food choices. Prepare nutritious meals at home using fresh ingredients and minimize reliance on processed and fast foods.

Breakfast

1. Everything Bagel Avocado Toast

Prep time: 5 minutes. | **Cook time:** 0 minutes. |
Serves: 2

Ingredients:

- 2 whole grain bread slices
- 1 ripe avocado
- 1 tablespoon lemon juice
- Everything bagel seasoning, to taste
- Black pepper, and salt, as required

Directions:

1. Toast the slices of bread to your desired level of crispness.
2. While the bread is toasting, cut the avocado in half and remove the pit.
3. Remove avocado flesh with a scoop and add to a bowl.
4. Mash the avocado with a fork until it reaches your desired consistency. Add lemon juice and season with black pepper, and salt, as required. Mix well.
5. Spread the mashed avocado evenly onto each slice of toasted bread.
6. Sprinkle a generous amount of everything bagel seasoning on top of the avocado layer.
7. Serve the everything bagel avocado toast immediately and enjoy!

Nutritional Information (per serving): Calories: 231; Fat: 20g; Sodium: 69mg; Carbs: 13.4g; Fibers: 7g; Sugar: 1.1g; Proteins: 2.7g

2. Banana Chocolate Chip Mini Muffins

Prep time: 5 minutes. | **Cook time:** 15 minutes. |
Serves: 6

Ingredients:

- 2 ripe bananas
- 2 large eggs
- ¼ cup honey
- 1 teaspoon vanilla extract
- ½ teaspoon baking soda
- ¼ teaspoon salt
- ½ cup creamy peanut butter
- ¼ cup unsweetened cocoa powder
- ¼ cup mini chocolate chips

Directions:

1. At 350°F (175°C), preheat your oven.
2. Grease any suitable mini muffin tin or line it with paper liners.
3. In a suitable-sized bowl, mash the ripe bananas with a fork until smooth.
4. Add the eggs, honey, vanilla extract, baking soda, salt, peanut butter or almond butter, and cocoa powder to the bowl with the mashed bananas. Mix until well combined and smooth.
5. If using, fold in the mini chocolate chips.
6. Spoon the batter into the prepared tin, filling each cavity roughly 2/3 full.
7. Bake them in your preheated oven for 10-12 minutes.
8. Remove the muffins from the oven and let them cool in the tin for a few minutes. Then transfer them to a wire rack to cool completely.
9. Enjoy these delightful, gluten-free mini muffins as a snack or for breakfast on the go!

Nutritional Information (per serving): Calories: 238; Fat: 13.1g; Sodium: 325mg; Carbs: 27g; Fibers: 3.5g; Sugar: 18.7g; Proteins: 8.7g

3. Two-Ingredient Banana Pancakes

Prep time: 5 minutes. | **Cook time:** 10 minutes. | **Serves:** 2

Ingredients:

- 2 ripe bananas
- 4 large eggs

Directions:

1. In a mixing bowl, mash the ripe bananas with a fork until they become a smooth paste.
2. Crack the eggs into the bowl with the mashed bananas.
3. Mix the bananas and eggs until well combined and the mixture is smooth.
4. Heat any suitable non-stick skillet or griddle over medium heat.
5. Pour a small amount of the prepared batter (about ¼ cup) onto the heated skillet for each pancake.
6. Cook for around 2-3 minutes, then flip the pancakes with a spatula.
7. Cook for a further 1-2 minutes.
8. Repeat with the remaining batter, adding more oil to the skillet if needed.
9. Serve the two-ingredient banana pancakes warm with your favorite toppings like fresh fruit, honey, or maple syrup.
10. Enjoy these simple and delicious pancakes that are gluten-free and have no added sugar!

Nutritional Information (per serving): Calories: 248; Fat: 10.3g; Sodium: 141mg; Carbs: 27.7g; Fibers: 3.1g; Sugar: 15.2g; Proteins: 13.9g

4. Breakfast Beans with Microwave-Poached Egg

Prep time: 10 minutes. | **Cook time:** 10 minutes. | **Serves:** 2

Ingredients:

- 1 can (15 oz.) canned beans, drained and rinsed
- ½ small onion, diced
- 1 clove garlic, minced
- ½ teaspoon (ground) cumin
- ½ teaspoon chili powder
- Black pepper, and salt, as required
- 1 tablespoon olive oil
- 1 large egg
- Chopped fresh cilantro, for garnish

Directions:

1. In a suitable-sized skillet, warm up the olive oil over medium heat. Toss in the diced onion and garlic mince, and sauté the onion for 5 minutes until translucent.
2. Add the drained and rinsed beans to the skillet, along with the ground cumin, chili powder, black pepper, and salt. Mix well to combine.
3. Cook the bean mixture for about 5 minutes, stir occasionally, until the beans are heated through and the flavors have melded together. If the mixture appears too dry, you can add a splash of water to moisten it.
4. Meanwhile, fill a microwave-safe bowl with about ½ cup of water. Carefully crack the egg into the bowl.
5. Place the bowl in the microwave and cook on high power for about 1-2 minutes.
6. Using any slotted spoon, remove the poached egg from the bowl, allowing any excess water to drain.
7. Serve the warm breakfast beans in a bowl, and gently place the poached egg on top.
8. Garnish with chopped fresh cilantro if desired.
9. Enjoy the protein-packed breakfast beans with a delicious microwave-poached egg!

Nutritional Information (per serving): Calories: 228; Fat: 11.3g; Sodium: 420mg; Carbs: 22.5g; Fibers: 7.4g; Sugar: 1.3g; Proteins: 10.5g

5. Southwestern Waffles

Prep time: 15 minutes. | **Cook time:** 15 minutes. | **Serves:** 4

Ingredients:

- 1 cup whole-wheat flour
- ½ cup cornmeal
- 1 tablespoon baking powder
- ½ teaspoon salt
- 1 teaspoon (ground) cumin
- ½ teaspoon chili powder
- 1 cup almond milk
- 2 large eggs
- 2 tablespoons almond butter, melted
- ½ cup corn kernels (fresh or canned)
- ¼ cup diced red bell pepper
- ¼ cup chopped green onions
- Cooking spray or additional melted almond butter, for greasing the waffle iron
- Sour cream, salsa, and sliced avocado, for serving

Directions:

1. Preheat your waffle iron as per manufacturer's instructions.
2. In a large mixing bowl, mix the flour, cornmeal, baking powder, salt, ground cumin, and chili powder.
3. In a separate bowl, mix the milk, eggs, and melted butter until well combined.
4. Pour the wet mixture into the bowl with the dry ingredients. Mix until just combined. Do not overmix; a few lumps are okay.
5. Gently fold in the corn kernels, diced red bell pepper, and chopped green onions.
6. Lightly grease the preheated waffle iron with cooking spray or melted butter.
7. Spoon the prepared batter onto the hot waffle iron, spreading it evenly. Close your waffle iron and cook until golden brown and crispy, following the instructions of your specific waffle iron.
8. Carefully remove the cooked waffle from the iron and keep it warm.
9. Repeat with the remaining batter, greasing the waffle iron as necessary.
10. Serve the Southwestern waffles warm with optional toppings sour cream, salsa, and sliced avocado.
11. Enjoy the savory and flavorful Southwestern waffles for a delicious breakfast or brunch!

Nutritional Information (per serving): Calories: 314; Fat: 10.8g; Sodium: 413mg; Carbs: 45.6g; Fibers: 3g; Sugar: 4.3g; Proteins: 10.6g

6. Pistachio & Peach Toast

Prep time: 10 minutes. | **Cook time:** 0 minutes. | **Serves:** 2

Ingredients:

- 2 whole-wheat bread slices, toasted
- 1 ripe peach, sliced
- 2 tablespoons low-fat cream cheese
- 2 tablespoons chopped pistachios
- Honey, for drizzling

Directions:

1. Spread a tablespoon of cream cheese onto each slice of toasted bread.
2. Arrange the peach slices on top of the cheese layer.
3. Sprinkle the chopped pistachios over the peaches.
4. Drizzle honey over the entire toast to add a touch of sweetness.
5. Serve the pistachio & peach toast immediately.
6. Enjoy this delightful and refreshing toast as a quick and tasty breakfast or snack!

Nutritional Information (per serving): Calories: 108; Fat: 5.7g; Sodium: 111mg; Carbs: 12.8g; Fibers: 1.8g; Sugar: 7.7g; Proteins: 2.9g

7. Sweet Potato Kale Breakfast Salad

Prep time: 15 minutes. | **Cook time:** 30 minutes. | **Serves:** 4

Ingredients:

- 2 cups kale, stems removed and chopped
- 1 medium-sized sweet potato, peeled & cubed
- 4 eggs
- 1 tablespoon olive oil
- ¼ cup sliced almonds
- ¼ cup dried cranberries
- Black pepper, and salt, as required
- **For the dressing:**
- 2 tablespoons olive oil
- 1 tablespoon apple cider vinegar
- 1 teaspoon honey
- 1 teaspoon Dijon mustard

Directions:

1. At 400°F (200°C), preheat your oven.
2. Spread the sweet potato cubes on a baking sheet, drizzle olive oil, and sprinkle with black pepper, and salt. Toss to coat evenly.
3. Roast these sweet potatoes in the oven for about 20-25 minutes.
4. While the sweet potatoes are roasting, prepare the dressing. In a suitable-sized bowl, mix the olive oil, apple cider vinegar, honey, and Dijon mustard until well combined. Set aside.
5. In a large skillet, warm up the tablespoon of olive oil over medium heat. Toss in the chopped kale and sauté for about 3-4 minutes until the kale is slightly wilted. Season with black pepper and salt to taste.
6. Fry the eggs in a separate nonstick pan to your liking (e.g., sunny-side-up, over-easy).
7. Once the sweet potatoes are ready, remove them from the oven and let them cool slightly.
8. In any rightly-sized salad bowl, mix the sautéed kale, roasted sweet potatoes, sliced almonds, and dried cranberries. Drizzle the prepared dressing over the salad and toss to coat everything evenly.
9. Divide the salad into individual bowls or plates. Top each serving with a fried egg. Season the eggs with black pepper, and salt, as required. Serve the sweet potato kale breakfast salad immediately and enjoy!

Nutritional Information (per serving): Calories: 210; Fat: 14.4g; Sodium: 101mg; Carbs: 13.2g; Fiber 2.5g; Sugars 4.2g; Protein 8.4g

8. Egg Tartine

Prep time: 10 minutes. | **Cook time:** 5 minutes. | **Serves:** 2

Ingredients:

- 2 whole wheat bread slices, toasted
- 2 large eggs
- 2 tablespoons almond butter
- Black pepper, and salt, as required
- Fresh herbs (parsley or chives), chopped

Directions:

1. In any suitable non-stick skillet, melt the butter over medium heat.
2. Carefully crack the eggs into the skillet, keeping them separate. Season with black pepper, and salt.
3. Cook the eggs sunny-side up or over-easy, depending on your preference. Cook until the whites are set.
4. While the eggs are cooking, place the toasted bread slices on a plate.
5. Once the eggs are cooked, carefully transfer each egg onto a slice of toasted bread.
6. Season the eggs with additional black pepper, and salt if desired.
7. Sprinkle the fresh herbs over the eggs for added flavor.
8. Serve the egg tartine immediately and enjoy the simple and delicious open-faced sandwich!

Nutritional Information (per serving): Calories: 197; Fat: 16.8g; Sodium: 213mg; Carbs: 5g; Fibers: 0.2g; Sugar: 0.8g; Proteins: 7.1g

9. Cannellini Bean & Herbed Ricotta Toast

Prep time: 10 minutes. | **Cook time:** 0 minutes. | **Serves:** 2

Ingredients:

- 2 whole wheat bread slices, toasted
- 1 cup cannellini beans, cooked and drained
- ½ cup low-fat ricotta cheese
- 2 tablespoons chopped fresh herbs
- 1 tablespoon lemon juice
- 1 tablespoon extra-virgin olive oil
- Black pepper, and salt, as required

Directions:

1. In a bowl, mix the cannellini beans, ricotta cheese, chopped fresh herbs, lemon juice, extra-virgin olive oil, black pepper, and salt. Mix well to combine.
2. Spread the bean and ricotta mixture onto each slice of toasted bread.
3. Drizzle additional olive oil and sprinkle with fresh herbs if desired.
4. Serve the cannellini bean and herbed ricotta toast immediately and enjoy the creamy and flavorful combination!

Nutritional Information (per serving): Calories: 282; Fat: 12.8g; Sodium: 471mg; Carbs: 28.5g; Fibers: 7.7g; Sugar: 3.1g; Proteins: 14.7g

10. Creamy Blueberry-Pecan Oatmeal

Prep time: 10 minutes. | **Cook time:** 10 minutes. | **Serves:** 2

Ingredients:

- 1 cup rolled oats
- 2 cups water
- Pinch of salt
- ½ cup blueberries (fresh or frozen)
- 2 tablespoons chopped pecans
- 2 tablespoons honey
- ¼ cup almond milk
- Fresh blueberries and chopped pecans for garnish

Directions:

1. In a saucepan, mix the rolled oats, water, and a pinch of salt. Bring to a boil over medium heat.
2. Reduce its heat to low and simmer for about 5-7 minutes, stir occasionally, until the oats are cooked and creamy.
3. Add the blueberries and chopped pecans to the oatmeal. Stir gently to combine and allow the blueberries to soften and release their juices.
4. Remove the saucepan from the heat and stir in the honey. Adjust the sweetness to your liking.
5. If desired, stir in the milk to make the oatmeal even creamier.
6. Serve the creamy blueberry-pecan oatmeal hot in bowls.
7. Garnish with blueberries and chopped pecans if desired.
8. Enjoy this comforting and nutritious oatmeal for a satisfying breakfast!

Nutritional Information (per serving): Calories: 352; Fat: 13.4g; Sodium: 103mg; Carbs: 53.8g; Fibers: 6.6g; Sugar: 23.1g; Proteins: 8.2g

Soups

11. Red Chilli & Bean Soup

Prep time: 15 minutes. | **Cook time:** 30 minutes. |
Serves: 4

Ingredients:

- 1 tablespoon olive oil
- 1 onion, diced
- 2 cloves garlic, minced
- 1 red bell pepper, diced
- 1 jalapeño pepper, seeds removed and finely chopped
- 1 teaspoon (ground) cumin
- 1 teaspoon chili powder
- ½ teaspoon paprika
- 1 can (14 oz.) diced tomatoes
- 2 cans (15 oz.) kidney beans, drained and rinsed
- 4 cups (low-sodium) vegetable broth
- Black pepper, and salt, as required
- Fresh cilantro, chopped (for garnish)
- Lime wedges (for serving)

Directions:

1. Warm up the olive oil in a large pot or Dutch oven over medium heat.
2. Toss in the diced onion, garlic mince, diced red bell pepper, and jalapeño pepper to the pot. Sauté until the vegetables are softened and fragrant, about 5 minutes.
3. Stir in the ground cumin, chili powder, and paprika. Cook for an additional minute to toast the spices.
4. Toss in the diced tomatoes, kidney beans, and vegetable broth to the pot. Mix well to combine.
5. Cook the soup to a boil, then reduce its heat and simmer for about 20-25 minutes, allowing the flavors to meld together.
6. Season with black pepper and salt to taste.
7. Divide the red chili & bean soup into bowls. Garnish with cilantro and serve with lime wedges on the side for squeezing over the soup.
8. Enjoy this hearty and spicy soup as a comforting meal!

Nutritional Information (per serving): Calories: 194;
Fat: 4.4g; Sodium: 84mg; Carbs: 36.4g; Fibers: 8.6g;
Sugar: 4.4g; Proteins: 29.1g

12. Mushroom and Lentil Soup

Prep time: 10 minutes. | **Cook time:** 50 minutes. |
Serves: 4

Ingredients:

- 1 tablespoon olive oil
- 1 onion, diced
- 2 cloves garlic, minced
- 8 oz. mushrooms, sliced
- 1 cup dried green lentils, rinsed
- 4 cups (low-sodium) vegetable broth
- 1 bay leaf
- 1 teaspoon dried thyme
- Black pepper, and salt, as required
- Fresh parsley, chopped (for garnish)

Directions:

1. Warm up the olive oil in a large pot or Dutch oven over medium heat.
2. Toss in the diced onion and garlic mince to the pot. Sauté the onion for about 5 minutes.
3. Add the sliced mushrooms to the pot and cook until they release their moisture and start to brown, about 8-10 minutes.
4. Stir in the dried green lentils, vegetable broth, bay leaf, and dried thyme. Cook the soup to a boil.
5. Reduce its heat to low, cover the pot, and simmer for about 30-35 minutes.
6. Season with black pepper and salt to taste.
7. Remove the bay leaf from the soup.
8. Divide the mushroom and lentil soup into bowls. Garnish with parsley.
9. Enjoy this wholesome and flavorful soup as a nourishing meal!

Nutritional Information (per serving): Calories: 264;
Fat: 5.6g; Sodium: 78mg; Carbs: 34.9g; Fibers: 15.9g;
Sugar: 3.8g; Proteins: 19.4g

13. Pea and Edamame Soup

Prep time: 10 minutes. | **Cook time:** 25 minutes. |
Serves: 4

Ingredients:

- 1 tablespoon olive oil
- 1 onion, diced
- 2 cloves garlic, minced
- 2 cups frozen peas
- 1 cup frozen edamame
- 4 cups (low-sodium) vegetable broth
- 1 teaspoon dried basil
- ½ teaspoon dried mint
- Black pepper, and salt, as required
- Fresh mint leaves, chopped (for garnish)

Directions:

1. Warm up the olive oil in a large pot or Dutch oven over medium heat.
2. Toss in the diced onion and garlic mince to the pot. Sauté the onion for about 5 minutes.
3. Add the frozen peas, frozen edamame, vegetable broth, dried basil, and dried mint to the pot. Mix well to combine.
4. Cook the soup to a boil, then reduce its heat and simmer for about 10-15 minutes, until the peas and edamame are cooked through.
5. Season with black pepper and salt to taste.
6. Puree the soup until it is smooth and creamy using an immersion blender or a tabletop blender.
7. When using a countertop blender, return the soup to the saucepan after mixing.
8. Reheat the soup over low heat if necessary.
9. Divide the pea and edamame soup into bowls. Garnish with mint leaves.
10. Enjoy this nutritious soup as a refreshing meal!

Nutritional Information (per serving): Calories: 214;
Fat: 8.6g; Sodium: 132mg; Carbs: 22.4g; Fibers: 6.6g;
Sugar: 5.9g; Proteins: 12.6g

14. Spiced Lentil and Carrot Soup

Prep time: 10 minutes. | **Cook time:** 30 minutes. |
Serves: 4

Ingredients:

- 1 tablespoon olive oil
- 1 onion, diced
- 2 cloves garlic, minced
- 2 carrots, peeled and chopped
- 1 cup dried red lentils, rinsed
- 4 cups (low-sodium) vegetable broth
- 1 teaspoon (ground) cumin
- ½ teaspoon (ground) coriander
- ¼ teaspoon turmeric
- Pinch of cayenne pepper
- Black pepper, and salt, as required
- Fresh cilantro, chopped (for garnish)

Directions:

1. Heat the olive oil in a suitable-sized pot or Dutch oven over medium heat.
2. Toss in the diced onion and garlic mince to the pot. Sauté the onion for about 5 minutes.
3. Toss in the chopped carrots and dried red lentils to the pot. Mix well to combine.
4. Pour in the vegetable broth, ground cumin, ground coriander, turmeric, and cayenne pepper. Stir again to combine.
5. Cook the soup to a boil, then reduce its heat and simmer for about 20-25 minutes.
6. Season with black pepper and salt to taste.
7. Using your immersion blender or a countertop blender, puree a portion of the soup to desired consistency. Leave some texture if desired.
8. When using a countertop blender, return the soup to the saucepan after mixing.
9. Reheat the soup over low heat if necessary.
10. Divide the spiced lentil and carrot soup into bowls. Garnish with cilantro.
11. Enjoy this comforting and aromatic soup as a satisfying meal!

Nutritional Information (per serving): Calories: 266;
Fat: 5.6g; Sodium: 189mg; Carbs: 36.1g; Fibers: 16.1g;
Sugar: 4.4g; Proteins: 18g

15. Warming Tomato Soup

Prep time: 10 minutes. | **Cook time:** 30 minutes. | **Serves:** 2

Ingredients:

- 2 tablespoons olive oil
- 1 onion, chopped
- 2 cloves garlic, minced
- 2 cans (14 oz.) diced tomatoes
- 2 cups (low-sodium) vegetable broth
- 1 teaspoon dried basil
- 1 teaspoon dried oregano
- ½ teaspoon paprika
- Black pepper, and salt, as required
- Fresh basil leaves, chopped (for garnish)

Directions:

1. Heat up the olive oil in a suitable-sized pot or Dutch oven over medium heat.
2. Toss in the chopped onion and garlic mince to the pot. Sauté the onion for about 5 minutes.
3. Toss in the diced tomatoes (including the liquid) to the pot. Mix well.
4. Pour in the vegetable broth and add the dried basil, dried oregano, paprika, black pepper, and salt. Stir to combine.
5. Cook the soup to a boil, then reduce its heat and simmer for about 20-25 minutes to allow the flavors to meld together.
6. Puree the soup until it is smooth and creamy using an immersion blender or a tabletop blender.
7. When using a countertop blender, return the soup to the saucepan after mixing.
8. Reheat the soup over low heat if necessary.
9. Divide the warming tomato soup into bowls. Garnish with basil leaves.
10. Enjoy this comforting and classic tomato soup on a chilly day!

Nutritional Information (per serving): Calories: 221; Fat: 16g; Sodium: 175mg; Carbs: 14.9g; Fibers: 3.9g; Sugar: 7.9g; Proteins: 7.4g

16. Butternut Squash and Sweet Potato Soup

Prep time: 10 minutes. | **Cook time:** 35 minutes. | **Serves:** 2

Ingredients:

- 1 butternut squash, peeled, seeded, and cubed
- 2 sweet potatoes, peeled and cubed
- 1 onion, chopped
- 2 cloves garlic, minced
- 4 cups (low-sodium) vegetable broth
- 1 teaspoon (ground) cinnamon
- ½ teaspoon (ground) nutmeg
- Black pepper, and salt, as required
- 2 tablespoons olive oil
- Toasted pumpkin seeds (for garnish)

Directions:

1. In a suitable-sized pot or Dutch oven, heat up the olive oil over medium heat.
2. Toss in the chopped onion and garlic mince to the pot. Sauté the onion for about 5 minutes.
3. Add the butternut squash, sweet potatoes, vegetable broth, (ground) cinnamon, ground nutmeg, black pepper, and salt to the pot. Mix well.
4. Cook the soup to a boil, then reduce its heat and simmer for about 20-25 minutes.
5. Puree the soup until it is smooth and creamy using an immersion blender or a tabletop blender.
6. When using a countertop blender, return the soup to the saucepan after mixing.
7. Reheat the soup over low heat if necessary.
8. Divide the butternut squash and sweet potato soup into bowls. Garnish with toasted pumpkin seeds.
9. Enjoy this velvety and comforting soup with the delightful flavors of fall!

Nutritional Information (per serving): Calories: 438; Fat: 17.4g; Sodium: 146mg; Carbs: 59.2g; Fibers: 9.5g; Sugar: 6.2g; Proteins: 13.6g

17. Carrot and Coriander Soup

Prep time: 10 minutes. | **Cook time:** 30 minutes. |
Serves: 4

Ingredients:

- 2 tablespoons olive oil
- 1 onion, chopped
- 2 cloves garlic, minced
- 6 large carrots, peeled and chopped
- 4 cups low-sodium vegetable broth
- 1 teaspoon (ground) coriander
- ½ teaspoon (ground) cumin
- Black pepper, and salt, as required
- Fresh coriander leaves, chopped (for garnish)

Directions:

1. Heat up the olive oil in a suitable-sized pot or Dutch oven over medium heat.
2. Toss in the chopped onion and minced garlic to the pot. Sauté the onion for about 5 minutes.
3. Toss in the chopped carrots to the pot. Mix well.
4. Pour in the vegetable broth and add the ground coriander, ground cumin, black pepper, and salt. Stir to combine.
5. Cook the soup to a boil, then reduce its heat and simmer for about 20-25 minutes.
6. Puree the soup until it is smooth and creamy using an immersion blender or a tabletop blender.
7. When using a countertop blender, return the soup to the saucepan after mixing.
8. Reheat the soup over low heat if necessary.
9. Divide the carrot and coriander soup into bowls. Garnish with coriander leaves.
10. Enjoy this aromatic soup packed with the goodness of carrots and coriander!

Nutritional Information (per serving): Calories: 157; Fat: 8.5g; Sodium: 139mg; Carbs: 14.7g; Fibers: 3.3g; Sugar: 7.2g; Proteins: 6.2g

18. Vegetable Weight-Loss Soup

Prep time: 15 minutes. | **Cook time:** 35 minutes. |
Serves: 4

Ingredients:

- 1 tablespoon olive oil
- 1 onion, chopped
- 2 cloves garlic, minced
- 2 carrots, peeled and chopped
- 2 stalks celery, chopped
- 1 bell pepper, chopped
- 1 zucchini, chopped
- 1 cup chopped green beans
- 4 cups (low-sodium) vegetable broth
- 1 can (14 oz.) diced tomatoes
- 1 teaspoon dried thyme
- 1 teaspoon dried rosemary
- Black pepper, and salt, as required
- Fresh parsley, chopped (for garnish)

Directions:

1. Heat up the olive oil in a suitable-sized pot or Dutch oven over medium heat.
2. Toss in the chopped onion and minced garlic to the pot. Sauté the onion for about 5 minutes.
3. Toss in the chopped carrots, celery, bell pepper, zucchini, and green beans to the pot. Mix well.
4. Pour in the vegetable broth and toss in the diced tomatoes (including the liquid), dried thyme, dried rosemary, black pepper, and salt. Stir to combine.
5. Cook the soup to a boil, then reduce its heat and simmer for about 20-25 minutes.
6. Season with additional black pepper, and salt, as required.
7. Divide the vegetable weight-loss soup into bowls. Garnish with parsley.
8. Enjoy this nourishing and low-calorie soup as part of a healthy and balanced diet!

Nutritional Information (per serving): Calories: 131; Fat: 5.3g; Sodium: 102mg; Carbs: 15.2g; Fibers: 4.2g; Sugar: 7.4g

19. Cream of Turkey & Wild Rice Soup

Prep time: 10 minutes. | **Cook time:** 25 minutes. | **Serves:** 4

Ingredients:

- 2 tablespoons almond butter
- 1 onion, diced
- 2 carrots, diced
- 2 stalks celery, diced
- 2 cloves garlic, minced
- ¼ cup whole-wheat flour
- 4 cups (low-sodium) chicken broth
- 2 cups cooked turkey, shredded or diced
- 1 cup cooked wild rice
- 1 cup low-fat cream
- Black pepper, and salt, as required
- Fresh parsley, chopped (for garnish)

Directions:

1. In a suitable-sized pot or Dutch oven, melt the butter over medium heat.
2. Toss in the diced onion, carrots, celery, and minced garlic to the pot. Sauté until the vegetables are softened, about 5 minutes.
3. Sprinkle the flour over the vegetables and stir to coat.
4. Gradually pour in the chicken broth, stirring constantly to prevent lumps.
5. Add the cooked turkey and cooked wild rice to the pot. Mix well to combine.
6. Cook the soup to a simmer and let it cook for about 10-15 minutes to allow the flavors to meld together.
7. Stir in the low-fat cream and season with black pepper and salt to taste.
8. Continue to simmer for an additional 5 minutes.
9. Divide the cream of turkey & wild rice soup into bowls. Garnish with parsley.
10. Enjoy this comforting and creamy soup, perfect for using up leftover turkey!

Nutritional Information (per serving): Calories: 386; Fat: 6.5g; Sodium: 284mg; Carbs: 45.8g; Fibers: 4.4g; Sugar: 6.1g; Proteins: 20.3g

20. Chicken & Spinach Soup with Pesto

Prep time: 10 minutes. | **Cook time:** 20 minutes. | **Serves:** 4

Ingredients:

- 2 cups fresh basil leaves
- ¼ cup low-fat parmesan cheese, grated
- ¼ cup pine nuts or walnuts
- 2 cloves garlic
- ¼ cup olive oil
- Black pepper, and salt, as required
- **For the Soup:**
- 1 tablespoon olive oil
- 1 onion, diced
- 2 carrots, diced
- 2 stalks celery, diced
- 2 cloves garlic, minced
- 6 cups (low-sodium) chicken broth
- 2 cups cooked chicken, shredded or diced
- 4 cups fresh spinach leaves
- Black pepper, and salt, as required
- Freshly grated Parmesan cheese (for garnish)

Directions:

1. For the Pesto: In a food processor or blender, mix the fresh basil leaves, grated Parmesan cheese, pine nuts or walnuts, and garlic.
2. Pulse until the ingredients are finely chopped. With the motor running, slowly drizzle in the olive oil until a smooth paste forms.
3. Season with black pepper, and salt. Set aside.
4. For the Soup: In a suitable-sized pot or Dutch oven, heat up the olive oil over medium heat.
5. Toss in the diced onion, carrots, celery, and minced garlic to the pot. Sauté until the vegetables are softened, about 5 minutes.
6. Pour in the chicken broth and bring it to a simmer.
7. Add the cooked chicken to the pot and let it cook for about 10 minutes to allow the flavors to blend.
8. Stir in the fresh spinach leaves and cook for an additional 2-3 minutes until wilted.
9. Season with black pepper, and salt.
10. Divide the chicken and spinach soup into bowls.
11. Top each bowl with a dollop of fresh pesto and a sprinkle of freshly grated Parmesan cheese.

Nutritional Information (per serving): Calories: 371; Fat: 13.2g; Sodium: 259mg; Carbs: 10.3g; Fibers: 2.7g; Sugar: 4.3g; Proteins: 31.2g

Salads & Sides

21. Grilled Chicken and Cherry Salad

Prep time: 10 minutes. | **Cook time:** 20 minutes. | **Serves:** 4

Ingredients:

- 2 boneless, skinless chicken breasts
- Black pepper, and salt, as required
- 6 cups mixed salad greens
- 1 cup fresh cherries, pitted and halved
- ½ cup crumbled low-fat feta cheese
- ¼ cup sliced almonds
- 2 tablespoons balsamic vinegar
- 2 tablespoons olive oil

Directions:

1. Preheat the grill to medium-high heat.
2. Season the chicken breasts with black pepper, and salt.
3. Grill the chicken for about 6-8 minutes per side.
4. Let it rest for a few minutes, then slice it into strips.
5. In a suitable-sized salad bowl, mix the mixed salad greens, fresh cherries, crumbled feta cheese, and sliced almonds.
6. In a suitable-sized bowl, mix the balsamic vinegar and olive oil to make the dressing.
7. Drizzle the prepared dressing over the salad and toss gently to coat.
8. Divide the salad among plates and top with the grilled chicken strips.
9. Serve the grilled chicken and cherry salad as a delicious and satisfying meal.

Nutritional Information (per serving): Calories: 322; Fat: 9.3g; Sodium: 326mg; Carbs: 11.4g; Fibers: 0.8g; Sugar: 1.1g; Proteins: 26.8g

22. Fresh Taco Salad

Prep time: 10 minutes. | **Cook time:** 10 minutes. | **Serves:** 4

Ingredients:

- 1 lb. (ground) lean beef or turkey
- 1 tablespoon olive oil
- 1 onion, chopped
- 2 cloves garlic, minced
- 1 tablespoon chili powder
- 1 teaspoon (ground) cumin
- ½ teaspoon paprika
- Black pepper, and salt, as required
- 4 cups shredded lettuce
- 1 cup cherry tomatoes, halved
- 1 cup canned black beans, rinsed and drained
- 1 cup frozen corn, thawed
- 1 avocado, diced
- ½ cup shredded low-fat cheddar cheese
- ¼ cup chopped fresh cilantro
- ¼ cup salsa
- ¼ cup low-fat sour cream

Directions:

1. In a suitable-sized skillet, heat up the olive oil over medium heat. Toss in the chopped onion and minced garlic, and cook until softened and fragrant, about 5 minutes.
2. Add the ground lean beef or turkey to the skillet and sauté until it is browned, crumbling it with a spoon as it cooks.
3. Stir in the chili powder, ground cumin, paprika, black pepper, and salt. To enable the flavors to mingle, cook for a further 2 to 3 minutes. Take it off the stove and put it aside.
4. In a suitable-sized salad bowl, mix the shredded lettuce, cherry tomatoes, black beans, corn, avocado, cheddar cheese, and fresh cilantro.
5. Add the cooked ground lean beef or turkey to the salad bowl and toss gently to combine.
6. Serve the fresh taco salad with salsa and sour cream on the side.

Nutritional Information (per serving): Calories: 449; Fat: 29.3g; Sodium: 252mg; Carbs: 31.5g; Fibers: 10.8g; Sugar: 5.2g; Proteins: 19.8g

23. Shrimp and Rice Noodle Salad

Prep time: 10 minutes. | **Cook time:** 20 minutes. |
Serves: 4

Ingredients:

- 8 oz. rice noodles
- 1 lb. shrimp, peeled and deveined
- 1 tablespoon olive oil
- Black pepper, and salt, as required
- 4 cups mixed salad greens
- 1 cucumber, thinly sliced
- 1 carrot, shredded
- ¼ cup chopped fresh cilantro
- ¼ cup chopped fresh mint
- ¼ cup chopped peanuts
- 2 tablespoons lime juice
- 1 tablespoon honey
- 1 clove garlic, minced
- 1 small red chili, thinly sliced

Directions:

1. Cook the rice noodles as per package instructions. Drain once cooked then set it aside.
2. In a suitable-sized skillet, heat up the olive oil over medium-high heat. Season the shrimp with black pepper, and salt, then add them to the skillet. Cook for about 2-3 minutes per side, until the shrimp are pink and cooked through. Remove it from the heat and let them cool slightly.
3. In a suitable-sized salad bowl, mix the mixed salad greens, cucumber slices, shredded carrot, chopped fresh cilantro, chopped fresh mint, and chopped peanuts.
4. In a suitable-sized bowl, mix the lime juice, honey, minced garlic, and red chili to make the dressing.
5. Add the cooked rice noodles and cooked shrimp to the salad bowl. Pour the dressing over the salad and toss gently to coat.
6. Serve the shrimp and rice noodle salad as a refreshing and satisfying meal.

Nutritional Information (per serving): Calories: 341;
Fat: 10.3g; Sodium: 350mg; Carbs: 31.5g; Fibers: 2.6g;
Sugar: 7g; Proteins: 31.8g

24. Indian Garbanzo Bean Salad with Pitas

Prep time: 40 minutes. | **Cook time:** 10 minutes. |
Serves: 4

Ingredients:

- 2 cans (15 oz.) garbanzo beans, rinsed and drained
- 1 cucumber, diced
- 1 bell pepper, diced
- ½ red onion, thinly sliced
- ¼ cup chopped fresh cilantro
- ¼ cup chopped fresh mint
- ¼ cup chopped roasted peanuts
- 2 tablespoons lemon juice
- 2 tablespoons olive oil
- 1 teaspoon (ground) cumin
- ½ teaspoon (ground) coriander
- ½ teaspoon paprika
- Black pepper, and salt, as required
- Pita bread, cut into wedges, for serving

Directions:

1. In a suitable-sized bowl, mix the garbanzo beans, diced cucumber, diced bell pepper, sliced red onion, chopped fresh cilantro, chopped fresh mint, and chopped roasted peanuts.
2. In a suitable-sized bowl, mix the lemon juice, olive oil, ground cumin, ground coriander, paprika, black pepper, and salt to make the dressing.
3. Pour the dressing over the garbanzo bean salad and toss gently to coat.
4. To allow the flavors to combine, let the salad marinate in the fridge for at least 30 minutes.
5. Serve the Indian garbanzo bean salad with pita bread wedges on the side.
6. Enjoy this flavorful and protein-packed salad with a touch of Indian-inspired spices!

Nutritional Information (per serving): Calories: 279;
Fat: 14g; Sodium: 15mg; Carbs: 31.1g; Fibers: 8.6g;
Sugar: 7.8g; Proteins: 10.9g

25.Maple Mahi-Mahi Salad

Prep time: 10 minutes. | **Cook time:** 10 minutes. |
Serves: 4

Ingredients:

- 2 mahi-mahi fillets
- 1 tablespoon maple syrup
- 2 tablespoons (low-sodium) soy sauce
- 1 tablespoon lemon juice
- Black pepper, and salt, as required
- 6 cups mixed salad greens
- 1 cup cherry tomatoes, halved
- ½ cup sliced cucumber
- ¼ cup sliced red onion
- ¼ cup chopped walnuts
- 2 tablespoons olive oil
- 1 tablespoon balsamic vinegar

Directions:

1. Preheat your grill or stovetop grill pan to medium-high heat.
2. In a suitable-sized bowl, mix the maple syrup, soy sauce, lemon juice, black pepper, and salt.
3. Brush the mahi-mahi fillets with the maple syrup mixture, making sure to coat both sides.
4. Grill the fillets for about 4-5 minutes per side. Remove it from the heat and let them rest for a few minutes.
5. In a suitable-sized salad bowl, mix the mixed salad greens, cherry tomatoes, cucumber, red onion, and walnuts.
6. In a separate small bowl, mix the olive oil and balsamic vinegar to make the dressing.
7. Drizzle the prepared dressing over the salad and toss to coat evenly.
8. Divide the salad onto plates and top each portion with a grilled mahi-mahi fillet.
9. Serve immediately and enjoy!

Nutritional Information (per serving): Calories: 222;
Fat: 11.9g; Sodium: 336mg; Carbs: 14.5g; Fibers: 1.4g;
Sugar: 5g; Proteins: 16.1g

26.Stone Fruit Salad with Baked Goat Cheese Coins

Prep time: 10 minutes. | **Cook time:** 10 minutes. |
Serves: 4

Ingredients:

- 4 oz. low-fat goat cheese
- ¼ cup breadcrumbs
- 2 tablespoons chopped fresh herbs
- 2 tablespoons olive oil
- 4 cups mixed salad greens
- 2 peaches, pitted and sliced
- 2 plums, pitted and sliced
- 1 cup blueberries
- ¼ cup sliced almonds
- Balsamic glaze, for drizzling

Directions:

1. At 375°F (190°C), preheat your oven.
2. Slice the goat cheese into 8 equal rounds.
3. In any right-sized shallow dish, mix the breadcrumbs and chopped herbs.
4. Dip each goat cheese round into the breadcrumb mixture, pressing gently to coat both sides.
5. Place the coated goat cheese rounds on a baking sheet and drizzle olive oil.
6. Bake it in your preheated oven for about 8-10 minutes.
7. In a suitable-sized salad bowl, mix the mixed salad greens, peach slices, plum slices, blueberries, and sliced almonds.
8. Drizzle the salad with balsamic glaze and toss gently to combine.
9. Divide the salad onto plates and top each portion with two baked goat cheese rounds.
10. Serve immediately and enjoy!

Nutritional Information (per serving): Calories: 338;
Fat: 21g; Sodium: 184mg; Carbs: 27.8g; Fibers: 3.8g;
Sugar: 15.4g; Proteins: 13.9g

27. Wilted Spinach Salad with Pears and Cranberries

Prep time: 10 minutes. | **Cook time:** 5 minutes. | **Serves:** 4

Ingredients:

- 6 cups fresh baby spinach
- 2 pears, cored and thinly sliced
- ½ cup dried cranberries
- ¼ cup crumbled feta cheese
- ¼ cup chopped walnuts
- 2 tablespoons olive oil
- 2 tablespoons balsamic vinegar
- 1 tablespoon honey
- Black pepper, and salt, as required

Directions:

1. Place the fresh baby spinach in a suitable-sized salad bowl.
2. Add the sliced pears, dried cranberries, crumbled feta cheese, and chopped walnuts to the bowl.
3. In a suitable-sized bowl, mix the olive oil, balsamic vinegar, honey, black pepper, and salt to make the dressing.
4. Heat a small skillet over medium heat and pour the dressing into the skillet.
5. Cook the dressing for about 1-2 minutes until warmed.
6. Pour the warm dressing over the salad and toss gently to wilt the spinach and coat all the ingredients.
7. Divide the salad onto plates and serve immediately.
8. Enjoy this delicious wilted spinach salad with pears and cranberries!

Nutritional Information (per serving): Calories: 229; Fat: 13.9g; Sodium: 142mg; Carbs: 24.4g; Fibers: 5.3g; Sugar: 15.7g; Proteins: 4.9g

28. Pan-Seared Pork and Fried Green Tomato Salad

Prep time: 15 minutes. | **Cook time:** 20 minutes. | **Serves:** 4

Ingredients:

- 2 boneless pork chops
- Black pepper, and salt, as required
- 2 green tomatoes, sliced
- ½ cup whole-wheat flour
- ¼ cup cornmeal
- 1 teaspoon paprika
- Vegetable oil, for frying
- 6 cups mixed salad greens
- ½ cup cherry tomatoes, halved
- ¼ cup thinly sliced red onion
- ¼ cup crumbled blue cheese
- 2 tablespoons olive oil
- 2 tablespoons balsamic vinegar

Directions:

1. Season the pork chops with black pepper and salt.
2. Heat a skillet over medium-high heat and add a small amount of oil.
3. Cook the pork chops for about 4-5 minutes per side until cooked through. Remove it from the heat and let them rest for a few minutes.
4. In any right-sixed shallow dish, mix the flour, cornmeal, paprika, black pepper, and salt.
5. Dip each green tomato slice into the flour mixture, pressing gently to coat both sides.
6. Heat vegetable oil in a separate skillet over medium-high heat for frying.
7. Fry the green tomato slices in batches for about 2-3 minutes per side until golden brown. Remove and drain on a paper towel.
8. In a suitable-sized salad bowl, mix the mixed salad greens, cherry tomatoes, red onion, and crumbled blue cheese.
9. In a suitable-sized bowl, mix the olive oil and balsamic vinegar to make the dressing.
10. Drizzle the prepared dressing over the salad and toss gently to coat.
11. Slice the cooked pork chops and place them on top of the salad.

Nutritional Information (per serving): Calories: 463; Fat: 16g; Sodium: 274mg; Carbs: 28.2g; Fibers: 2.1g; Sugar: 2.1g; Proteins: 50.9g

29.Wilted Spinach and Tilapia Salad

Prep time: 10 minutes. | **Cook time:** 10 minutes. |
Serves: 4

Ingredients:

- 2 tilapia fillets
- Black pepper, and salt, as required
- 6 cups fresh baby spinach
- ½ cup cherry tomatoes, halved
- ¼ cup sliced red onion
- ¼ cup crumbled feta cheese
- 2 tablespoons olive oil
- 2 tablespoons lemon juice
- 1 clove garlic, minced

Directions:

1. Season the tilapia fillets with black pepper, and salt on both sides.
2. Heat a skillet over medium-high heat and add a small amount of oil.
3. Cook the tilapia fillets for about 3-4 minutes per side until cooked through. Remove it from the heat and let them rest for a few minutes.
4. In the same skillet, add the olive oil and garlic mince. Sauté for about 1 minute until fragrant.
5. Add the baby spinach to the skillet and toss gently until wilted.
6. In a suitable-sized salad bowl, mix the wilted spinach, cherry tomatoes, red onion, and crumbled feta cheese.
7. In a suitable-sized bowl, mix the olive oil, lemon juice, black pepper, and salt to make the dressing.
8. Drizzle the prepared dressing over the salad and toss gently to coat.
9. Break the cooked tilapia fillets into bite-sized pieces and add them to the salad.
10. Serve immediately and enjoy!

Nutritional Information (per serving): Calories: 175; Fat: 10.3g; Sodium: 173mg; Carbs: 4g; Fibers: 1.5g; Sugar: 1.6g; Proteins: 19g

30.Shrimp and Watercress Salad

Prep time: 10 minutes. | **Cook time:** 0 minutes. |
Serves: 4

Ingredients:

- 1 lb. cooked shrimp, peeled and deveined
- 4 cups watercress, tough stems removed
- 1 cup cherry tomatoes, halved
- ½ cup red onion, thinly sliced
- 1 avocado, sliced
- ¼ cup chopped fresh cilantro
- 2 tablespoons lemon juice
- 2 tablespoons extra-virgin olive oil
- Black pepper, and salt, as required

Directions:

1. In a suitable-sized bowl, combine watercress, cherry tomatoes, red onion, avocado, and cilantro.
2. In a suitable-sized bowl, mix lemon juice, olive oil, black pepper, and salt.
3. Add the cooked shrimp to the large bowl and drizzle the prepared dressing over the salad.
4. Toss gently to coat everything evenly.
5. Serve it immediately and enjoy!

Nutritional Information (per serving): Calories: 320; Fat: 19.1g; Sodium: 306mg; Carbs: 9.4g; Fibers: 4.7g; Sugar: 2.3g; Proteins: 28.4g

31. Gingered Beef and Broccoli Salad Bowl

Prep time: 10 minutes. | **Cook time:** 5 minutes. | **Serves:** 6

Ingredients:

- 1 lb. beef sirloin, thinly sliced
- 3 cups broccoli florets
- 2 cups cooked quinoa
- 1 red bell pepper, thinly sliced
- ½ cup shredded carrots
- ¼ cup sliced green onions
- 2 tablespoons (low-sodium) soy sauce
- 1 tablespoon honey
- 1 tablespoon grated fresh ginger
- 2 tablespoons rice vinegar
- 2 tablespoons sesame oil
- Black pepper, and salt, as required

Directions:

1. In a suitable-sized skillet, heat some oil over medium-high heat. Add the beef slices and cook until browned. Remove it from the heat and set aside.
2. In a pot of boiling water, blanch the broccoli florets for 2-3 minutes until crisp-tender. Drain and rinse with cold water.
3. In a suitable-sized bowl, mix the cooked quinoa, blanched broccoli, red bell pepper, shredded carrots, and green onions.
4. In a suitable-sized bowl, mix soy sauce, honey, grated ginger, rice vinegar, sesame oil, black pepper, and salt.
5. Add the cooked beef to the bowl of vegetables and drizzle the prepared dressing over the top.
6. Toss gently to combine all the ingredients and coat them with the dressing.
7. Serve the gingered beef and broccoli salad bowl immediately and enjoy!

Nutritional Information (per serving): Calories: 436; Fat: 12.9g; Sodium: 376mg; Carbs: 46g; Fibers: 5.9g; Sugar: 5.3g; Proteins: 33g

32. Mediterranean Chicken Salad

Prep time: 10 minutes. | **Cook time:** 10 minutes. | **Serves:** 4

Ingredients:

- 2 boneless, skinless chicken breasts
- 4 cups mixed salad greens
- 1 cup cherry tomatoes, halved
- ½ cup cucumber, diced
- ¼ cup sliced Kalamata olives
- ¼ cup crumbled feta cheese
- 2 tablespoons chopped fresh parsley
- 2 tablespoons lemon juice
- 2 tablespoons red wine vinegar
- ¼ cup extra-virgin olive oil
- 1 teaspoon dried oregano
- Black pepper, and salt, as required

Directions:

1. Season the chicken breasts with black pepper, and salt. Grill or cook them in a suitable-sized skillet over medium-high heat until cooked through. Allow the chicken to cool slightly, then slice it into thin strips.
2. In a suitable-sized bowl, mix the mixed salad greens, cherry tomatoes, cucumber, Kalamata olives, crumbled feta cheese, and chopped parsley.
3. In a suitable-sized bowl, mix lemon juice, red wine vinegar, olive oil, dried oregano, black pepper, and salt.
4. Add the sliced chicken to the bowl of vegetables and drizzle the prepared dressing over the top.
5. Toss gently to mix everything and coat them with the dressing.
6. Serve the Mediterranean chicken salad with Greek dressing immediately and enjoy!

Nutritional Information (per serving): Calories: 313; Fat: 21g; Sodium: 280mg; Carbs: 8.2g; Fibers: 1.1g; Sugar: 2g; Proteins: 24g

33. Carrot and Avocado Salad

Prep time: 10 minutes. | **Cook time:** 0 minutes. |
Serves: 2

Ingredients:

- 2 large carrots, peeled and grated
- 1 ripe avocado, peeled, pitted, and diced
- ¼ cup chopped fresh cilantro
- 2 tablespoons lemon juice
- 2 tablespoons extra-virgin olive oil
- ¼ teaspoon cumin powder
- Black pepper, and salt, as required

Directions:

1. In a suitable-sized bowl, mix the grated carrots, diced avocado, and chopped cilantro.
2. In a suitable-sized bowl, mix lemon juice, olive oil, cumin powder, black pepper, and salt.
3. Pour the dressing over the carrot and avocado mixture.
4. Toss gently to coat all the ingredients evenly.
5. Serve the carrot and avocado salad immediately and enjoy!

Nutritional Information (per serving): Calories: 360;
Fat: 33.8g; Sodium: 60mg; Carbs: 16.2g; Fibers: 8.7g;
Sugar: 4.4g; Proteins: 2.7g

34. Arugula, Avocado, and Tomato Salad

Prep time: 10 minutes. | **Cook time:** 0 minutes. |
Serves: 4

Ingredients:

- 4 cups arugula
- 1 ripe avocado, peeled, pitted, and sliced
- 1 cup cherry tomatoes, halved
- ¼ cup sliced red onion
- 2 tablespoons lemon juice
- 2 tablespoons extra-virgin olive oil
- 1 tablespoon balsamic vinegar
- Black pepper, and salt, as required

Directions:

1. In a suitable-sized bowl, mix the arugula, avocado slices, cherry tomatoes, and sliced red onion.

2. In a suitable-sized bowl, mix lemon juice, olive oil, balsamic vinegar, black pepper, and salt.
3. Drizzle the prepared dressing over the salad.
4. Toss gently to coat all the ingredients with the dressing.
5. Serve the arugula, avocado, and tomato salad immediately and enjoy!

Nutritional Information (per serving): Calories: 181;
Fat: 17.1g; Sodium: 13mg; Carbs: 7.7g; Fibers: 4.4g;
Sugar: 2.3g; Proteins: 2g

35. Broccoli Salad with Apples and Cranberries

Prep time: 10 minutes. | **Cook time:** 5 minutes. |
Serves: 4

Ingredients:

- 4 cups broccoli florets
- 1 apple, cored and diced
- ¼ cup dried cranberries
- ¼ cup chopped walnuts
- 2 tablespoons lemon juice
- 2 tablespoons Greek yogurt
- 1 tablespoon honey
- 1 tablespoon apple cider vinegar
- Black pepper, and salt, as required

Directions:

1. In a pot of boiling water, blanch the broccoli florets for 2-3 minutes until crisp-tender. Drain and rinse with cold water.
2. In a suitable-sized bowl, mix the blanched broccoli florets, diced apple, dried cranberries, and chopped walnuts.
3. In a suitable-sized bowl, mix lemon juice, Greek yogurt, honey, apple cider vinegar, black pepper, and salt.
4. Drizzle the prepared dressing over the salad and toss gently to coat all the ingredients.
5. Serve the super-nutritious broccoli salad with apples and cranberries immediately and enjoy!

Nutritional Information (per serving): Calories: 206;
Fat: 7.1g; Sodium: 65mg; Carbs: 23.7g; Fibers: 4.5g;
Sugar: 16.2g; Proteins: 14.7g

Meat & Poultry

36. Chicken, Brussels Sprouts & Mushrooms One-Pot Pasta

Prep time: 10 minutes. | **Cook time:** 10 minutes. | **Serves:** 4

Ingredients:

- 1 lb. chicken breast, cut into bite-sized pieces
- 8 oz. mushrooms, sliced
- 1 lb. Brussels sprouts, trimmed and halved
- 8 oz. penne pasta
- 4 cloves garlic, minced
- 1 onion, finely chopped
- 4 cups (low-sodium) chicken broth
- 1 cup low-fat cream
- ½ cup low-fat parmesan cheese, grated
- 2 tablespoons olive oil
- 1 teaspoon dried thyme
- Black pepper, and salt, to taste
- Fresh parsley, chopped (for garnish)

Directions:

1. In a suitable-sized pot or Dutch oven, heat olive oil over medium heat. Add the chicken and cook until browned on all sides. Remove the chicken from the pot and set aside.
2. In the same pot, add the onion and garlic. Sauté for 2-3 minutes until fragrant and translucent. Add the mushrooms and Brussels sprouts, and cook for another 5 minutes until they start to soften.
3. Return the chicken to the pot and add the dried thyme, black pepper, and salt. Stir to combine.
4. Pour in the chicken broth and bring it to a boil. Add the penne pasta and cook as per package instructions until al dente, stir occasionally.
5. Reduce its heat to low and stir in the low-fat cream and grated Parmesan cheese. Simmer for 2-3 minutes until the sauce thickens slightly.
6. Taste and adjust the seasoning if needed. Remove it from the heat and let it rest for a few minutes.
7. Serve the one-pot pasta hot, garnished with fresh parsley. Enjoy!

Nutritional Information (per serving): Calories: 514; Fat: 16g; Sodium: 234mg; Carbs: 54g; Fibers: 5.6g; Sugar: 5.4g; Proteins: 41g

37. Honey-Roasted Chicken Thighs with Sweet Potato Wedges

Prep time: 10 minutes. | **Cook time:** 35 minutes. | **Serves:** 4

Ingredients:

- 4 chicken thighs
- 2 large sweet potatoes, peeled and cut into wedges
- 1 lb. Brussels sprouts, trimmed and halved
- 2 tablespoons honey
- 2 tablespoons Dijon mustard
- 2 tablespoons olive oil
- 2 cloves garlic, minced
- 1 teaspoon dried thyme
- Black pepper, and salt, to taste
- Fresh parsley, chopped (for garnish)

Directions:

1. At 400°F (200°C), preheat your oven. Line a baking sheet with parchment paper.
2. In a suitable-sized bowl, mix the honey, Dijon mustard, olive oil, garlic mince, dried thyme, black pepper, and salt.
3. Place the chicken thighs, sweet potato wedges, and Brussels sprouts on the prepared baking sheet. Drizzle the honey mixture over the chicken and vegetables, making sure to coat them evenly.
4. Roast for 30-35 minutes in a preheated oven.
5. Remove from the oven and let it cool for a few minutes. Garnish with parsley.
6. Serve the roasted chicken thighs with sweet potato wedges and Brussels sprouts hot. Enjoy!

Nutritional Information (per serving): Calories: 498; Fat: 18.3g; Sodium: 245mg; Carbs: 39g; Fibers: 7.7g; Sugar: 8.9g; Proteins: 46g

38. Slow-Cooked Ranch Chicken and Vegetables

Prep time: 10 minutes. | **Cook time:** 8 hrs. | **Serves:** 4

Ingredients:

- 4 boneless, skinless chicken breasts
- 1 lb. baby red potatoes, quartered
- 2 cups baby carrots
- 1 cup frozen green beans
- 1 packet ranch seasoning mix
- 1 cup (low-sodium) chicken broth
- ½ cup low-fat sour cream
- 2 tablespoons whole-wheat flour
- Black pepper, and salt, to taste
- Fresh parsley, chopped (for garnish)

Directions:

1. Season the chicken breasts with black pepper, and salt. Place them in the slow cooker.
2. Add the baby red potatoes, baby carrots, and frozen green beans to the slow cooker, arranging them around the chicken.
3. In a suitable-sized bowl, mix the ranch seasoning mix and chicken broth. Pour the mixture over the chicken and vegetables in the slow cooker.
4. Cover the slow cooker and cook on low heat for 6-8 hours, or on high heat for 3-4 hours, until the chicken is cooked through and the vegetables are tender.
5. In a separate bowl, mix the sour cream and flour until smooth. Stir the mixture into the slow cooker during the last 30 minutes of cooking to thicken the sauce.
6. Once the cooking time is complete, remove the chicken and vegetables from the slow cooker and transfer them to a serving platter.
7. Garnish with parsley and serve the slow-cooked ranch chicken and vegetables hot, spooning the sauce over the chicken. Enjoy!

Nutritional Information (per serving): Calories: 434; Fat: 16.6g; Sodium: 171mg; Carbs: 24g; Fibers: 2.8g; Sugar: 2.1g; Proteins: 44.9g

39. Skillet Lemon Chicken & Potatoes with Kale

Prep time: 10 minutes. | **Cook time:** 20 minutes. | **Serves:** 4

Ingredients:

- 4 boneless, skinless chicken breasts
- 1 lb. baby potatoes, halved
- 4 cups kale, stems removed and roughly chopped
- 2 lemons, zested and juiced
- 4 cloves garlic, minced
- 2 tablespoons olive oil
- 1 teaspoon dried thyme
- Black pepper, and salt, to taste

Directions:

1. Season the chicken breasts with black pepper, salt, and dried thyme.
2. In a suitable-sized skillet, heat olive oil over medium-high heat. Add the chicken breasts and cook for about 6-8 minutes per side. Remove the chicken from the skillet and set aside.
3. In the same skillet, add the halved baby potatoes and garlic mince. Cook for about 8-10 minutes, stir occasionally, until the potatoes are golden brown and crispy.
4. Return the chicken breasts to the skillet, placing them on top of the potatoes. Toss in the chopped kale, lemon zest, lemon juice, and a sprinkle of black pepper, and salt.
5. Cover the skillet and reduce its heat to medium-low. Let it cook for another 5-7 minutes.
6. Remove it from the heat and serve the skillet lemon chicken and potatoes with kale hot. Garnish with additional lemon zest. Enjoy!

Nutritional Information (per serving): Calories: 438; Fat: 17.6g; Sodium: 162mg; Carbs: 25g; Fibers: 4.8g; Sugar: 0.8g; Proteins: 45.9g

40. Garlic Cashew Chicken Casserole

Prep time: 10 minutes. | **Cook time:** 40 minutes. | **Serves:** 6

Ingredients:

- 4 boneless, skinless chicken breasts, cut into bite-sized pieces
- 1 cup cashews, unsalted
- 4 cups cooked rice
- 1 cup frozen peas
- 4 cloves garlic, minced
- 1 onion, finely chopped
- 2 tablespoons (low-sodium) soy sauce
- 2 tablespoons vegetable oil
- Black pepper, and salt, to taste
- Fresh cilantro, chopped (for garnish)

Directions:

1. At 375°F (190°C), preheat your oven. Grease a casserole dish with vegetable oil or cooking spray.
2. In a suitable-sized skillet, heat vegetable oil over medium-high heat. Toss in the chopped onion and garlic mince. Sauté for 2-3 minutes until fragrant and translucent.
3. Add the chicken pieces to the skillet and cook until browned on all sides. Season with black pepper, and salt.
4. In a separate small skillet, toast the cashews over medium heat until lightly golden. Remove it from the heat and set aside.
5. In the greased casserole dish, layer the cooked rice, cooked chicken and onion mixture, frozen peas, and toasted cashews. Drizzle the soy sauce evenly over the top.
6. Cover the casserole dish with foil and bake it in your preheated oven for 20-25 minutes.
7. Remove from the oven and let it cool for a few minutes. Garnish with cilantro.
8. Serve the garlic cashew chicken casserole hot. Enjoy!

Nutritional Information (per serving): Calories: 495; Fat: 23g; Sodium: 266mg; Carbs: 37.9g; Fibers: 3.5g; Sugar: 4.7g; Proteins: 34.7g

41. Roast Chicken & Sweet Potatoes

Prep time: 10 minutes. | **Cook time:** 1 hr. 15 minutes. | **Serves:** 4

Ingredients:

- 1 whole chicken (about 4 lbs./1.8kg)
- 2 large sweet potatoes, peeled and cut into chunks
- 1 onion, quartered
- 4 cloves garlic, minced
- 2 tablespoons olive oil
- 1 teaspoon dried rosemary
- 1 teaspoon dried thyme
- Black pepper, and salt, to taste
- Fresh parsley, chopped (for garnish)

Directions:

1. At 425°F (220°C), preheat your oven. Place a roasting rack in a roasting pan or baking sheet.
2. Rinse the chicken inside and out, then pat it dry with paper towels. Place the chicken on the roasting rack.
3. In a suitable-sized bowl, mix garlic mince, olive oil, dried rosemary, dried thyme, black pepper, and salt. Rub the mixture all over the chicken, including the cavity.
4. In a suitable-sized bowl, toss the sweet potato chunks and quartered onion with olive oil, black pepper, and salt.
5. Arrange the sweet potato chunks and onion quarters around the chicken on the roasting rack.
6. Roast the chicken and sweet potatoes in your preheated oven for about 1 hour and 15 minutes, basting the chicken with pan juices every 20-30 minutes.
7. Remove from the oven and let it rest for a few minutes. Garnish with parsley.
8. Carve the roast chicken and serve with the roasted sweet potatoes. Enjoy!

Nutritional Information (per serving): Calories: 235; Fat: 10g; Sodium: 40mg; Carbs: 24.8g; Fibers: 4g; Sugar: 1.6g; Proteins: 12.2g

42. Beef Stir-Fry with Baby Bok Choy & Ginger

Prep time: 10 minutes. | **Cook time:** 15 minutes. | **Serves:** 2

Ingredients:

- 1 lb. beef steak, thinly sliced
- 4 baby bok choy, ends trimmed and leaves separated
- 1 red bell pepper, thinly sliced
- 1 onion, thinly sliced
- 2 cloves garlic, minced
- 1 tablespoon fresh ginger, grated
- 3 tablespoons (low-sodium) soy sauce
- 1 tablespoon sesame oil
- 2 tablespoons vegetable oil
- Black pepper, and salt, to taste
- Sesame seeds, for garnish

Directions:

1. In a suitable-sized bowl, combine soy sauce, sesame oil, garlic mince, and grated ginger. Set aside.
2. Heat vegetable oil in a suitable-sized skillet or wok over high heat. Add the sliced beef and stir-fry for about 2-3 minutes until browned. Take the steak from the skillet and put aside.
3. Red bell pepper and onion slices should be added to the same skillet. Stir-frying for 2-3 minutes, or until they begin to soften.
4. Add the baby bok choy leaves to the skillet and stir-fry for another 2 minutes until wilted.
5. Return the beef to the skillet and pour the sauce mixture over the ingredients. Stir-fry for an additional 2 minutes, making sure everything is well coated in the sauce.
6. Season with black pepper and salt to taste. Remove it from the heat.
7. Transfer the beef stir-fry to a serving dish and garnish with sesame seeds.
8. Serve the beef stir-fry with baby bok choy and ginger hot over steamed rice or noodles. Enjoy!

Nutritional Information (per serving): Calories: 341; Fat: 17.5g; Sodium: 431mg; Carbs: 6.6g; Fibers: 6.8g; Sugar: 10.8g; Proteins: 35.3g

43. Lemon-Garlic Steak & Green Beans

Prep time: 15 minutes. | **Cook time:** 15 minutes. | **Serves:** 4

Ingredients:

- 4 lean steak cuts (ribeye, sirloin, or flank steak)
- 1 lb. green beans, trimmed
- 4 cloves garlic, minced
- 2 lemons, zested and juiced
- 2 tablespoons olive oil
- 2 tablespoons almond butter
- Black pepper, and salt, to taste
- Fresh parsley, chopped (for garnish)

Directions:

1. Preheat the grill or grill pan to medium-high heat.
2. Season the steak cuts with black pepper, salt, and garlic mince. Set aside.
3. In a suitable-sized pot of boiling salted water, blanch the green beans for 3-4 minutes until bright green and slightly tender. Drain once cooked then set it aside.
4. In a suitable-sized bowl, mix lemon zest, lemon juice, olive oil, black pepper, and salt.
5. Place the seasoned steak cuts on the preheated grill or grill pan. Cook for about 4-6 minutes per side. Remove the steaks from the grill and let them rest for a few minutes.
6. In a suitable-sized skillet over medium heat, melt the butter. Add the blanched green beans and sauté for 2-3 minutes until heated through.
7. Pour the lemon-oil mixture over the green beans and toss to coat evenly.
8. Slice the rested steaks and serve them alongside the lemon-garlic green beans. Garnish with parsley.
9. Serve the lemon-garlic steak and green beans hot. Enjoy!

Nutritional Information (per serving): Calories: 317; Fat: 18.3g; Sodium: 105mg; Carbs: 11.8g; Fibers: 4.7g; Sugar: 2.4g; Proteins: 28.5g

44. Skillet Steak with Mushroom Sauce

Prep time: 15 minutes. | **Cook time:** 15 minutes. |
Serves: 2

Ingredients:

- 2 steak cuts (ribeye, sirloin, or filet mignon)
- 8 oz. mushrooms, sliced
- 1 small onion, finely chopped
- 2 cloves garlic, minced
- 1 cup (low-sodium) beef broth
- ½ cup low-fat cream
- 2 tablespoons almond butter
- 2 tablespoons olive oil
- 1 tablespoon whole-wheat flour
- Black pepper, and salt, to taste
- Fresh thyme leaves, for garnish

Directions:

1. Season the steak cuts with black pepper, and salt.
2. In a suitable-sized skillet over medium-high heat, melt the butter with olive oil. Add the seasoned steaks and cook for about 4-6 minutes per side. Remove the steaks from the skillet and let them rest for a few minutes.
3. In the same skillet, add the sliced mushrooms and chopped onion. Sauté for about 5 minutes until the mushrooms release their moisture and start to brown.
4. Add the garlic mince to the skillet and cook for an additional minute until fragrant.
5. Sprinkle the flour over the mushrooms, onions, and garlic. Stir to coat evenly.
6. Slowly pour in the beef broth, stirring constantly to avoid lumps. Cook the mixture to a simmer and let it cook for about 3-4 minutes until the sauce thickens slightly.
7. Stir in the low-fat cream and season with black pepper and salt to taste. Cook for another 2 minutes to heat the sauce through.
8. Slice the rested steaks and serve them with the mushroom sauce poured over the top. Garnish with thyme leaves.
9. Serve the skillet steak with mushroom sauce hot with your choice of side dishes. Enjoy!

Nutritional Information (per serving): Calories: 511; Fat: 33g; Sodium: 316mg; Carbs: 20.3g; Fibers: 2.1g; Sugar: 3.9g; Proteins: 37g

45. Baked Beans with Ground lean beef

Prep time: 15 minutes. | **Cook time:** 45 minutes. |
Serves: 4

Ingredients:

- 1 lb. (ground) lean beef
- 2 cans (15 oz.) baked beans
- ½ cup ketchup
- 2 tablespoons brown sugar
- 1 tablespoon mustard
- 1 onion, finely chopped
- 2 cloves garlic, minced
- 2 tablespoons vegetable oil
- Black pepper, and salt, to taste
- Optional toppings: chopped green onions

Directions:

1. At 350°F (175°C), preheat your oven.
2. In a suitable-sized skillet, heat vegetable oil over medium heat. Toss in the chopped onion and garlic mince. Sauté for 2-3 minutes until fragrant and translucent.
3. Add the ground lean beef to the skillet and cook until browned, breaking it up into crumbles. Season with black pepper, and salt.
4. In a baking dish, mix the baked beans, ketchup, brown sugar, and mustard. Stir in the cooked ground lean beef mixture.
5. Cover the baking dish with foil and bake it in your preheated oven for 30-40 minutes.
6. Remove from the oven and let it cool for a few minutes. Sprinkle chopped green onions on top.
7. Serve the baked beans with ground lean beef hot as a side dish or as a main course. Enjoy!

Nutritional Information (per serving): Calories: 403; Fat: 16.9g; Sodium: 899mg; Carbs: 43.1g; Fibers: 8.1g; Sugar: 12.6g; Proteins: 21.6g

46. Balsamic Pork Tenderloin

Prep time: 40 minutes. | **Cook time:** 25 minutes. | **Serves:** 2

Ingredients:

- 2 pork tenderloins (about 1 lb.)
- ¼ cup balsamic vinegar
- 2 tablespoons (low-sodium) soy sauce
- 2 tablespoons honey
- 2 cloves garlic, minced
- 1 tablespoon Dijon mustard
- 1 tablespoon olive oil
- Black pepper, and salt, to taste
- Fresh rosemary or thyme sprigs, for garnish

Directions:

1. At 400°F (200°C), preheat your oven.
2. In a suitable-sized bowl, mix balsamic vinegar, soy sauce, honey, garlic mince, Dijon mustard, olive oil, black pepper, and salt.
3. Place the pork tenderloins in a baking dish or a resealable plastic bag. Pour the balsamic marinade over the pork, making sure it is well coated. Let it marinate for at least 30 minutes, or up to overnight in the refrigerator.
4. Heat a suitable-sized oven-safe skillet over medium-high heat. Remove the pork tenderloins from the marinade (reserving the marinade) and sear them in the hot skillet for about 2-3 minutes per side until browned.
5. Pour the reserved marinade into the skillet with the pork tenderloins. Transfer the skillet to the preheated oven.
6. Roast the pork tenderloins for about 15-20 minutes.
7. Remove the skillet from the oven and let the pork rest for a few minutes before slicing.
8. Slice the rested pork tenderloins and serve them hot, garnished with fresh rosemary or thyme sprigs.
9. Serve the balsamic pork tenderloin with your choice of side dishes. Enjoy!

Nutritional Information (per serving): Calories: 301; Fat: 13.5g; Sodium: 600mg; Carbs: 20.2g; Fibers: 0.5g; Sugar: 17.7g; Proteins: 24.3g

47. Sesame-Garlic Beef & Broccoli with Whole-Wheat Noodles

Prep time: 15 minutes. | **Cook time:** 25 minutes. | **Serves:** 2

Ingredients:

- 1 lb. beef sirloin or flank steak, thinly sliced
- 4 cups broccoli florets
- 8 oz. whole-wheat noodles
- 4 cloves garlic, minced
- 2 tablespoons (low-sodium) soy sauce
- 1 tablespoon sesame oil
- 1 tablespoon vegetable oil
- 1 tablespoon cornstarch (for thickening the sauce)
- 1 tablespoon sesame seeds, for garnish
- Black pepper, and salt, to taste

Directions:

1. Cook the whole-wheat noodles as per package instructions. Drain once cooked then set it aside.
2. In a suitable-sized bowl, mix soy sauce, sesame oil, garlic mince, and cornstarch. Set aside.
3. Heat vegetable oil in a suitable-sized skillet or wok over high heat. Add the sliced beef and stir-fry for about 2-3 minutes until browned. Remove the beef from the skillet and set aside.
4. In the same skillet, add the broccoli florets. Stir-fry for about 4-5 minutes until crisp-tender.
5. Return the beef to the skillet with the broccoli. Pour the sauce mixture over the ingredients.
6. Continue stir-frying for another 2-3 minutes until the sauce thickens and coats the beef and broccoli. Season with black pepper and salt to taste.
7. Add the cooked whole-wheat noodles to the skillet and toss everything to combine.
8. Remove it from the heat and transfer the sesame-garlic beef and broccoli with whole-wheat noodles to a serving dish.
9. Garnish with sesame seeds and serve hot. Enjoy!

Nutritional Information (per serving): Calories: 518; Fat: 17g; Sodium: 566mg; Carbs: 43.3g; Fibers: 9g; Sugar: 3.4g; Proteins: 48g

48. Lamb Chops with Mint Pan Sauce

Prep time: 15 minutes. | **Cook time:** 20 minutes. | **Serves:** 4

Ingredients:

- 4 lamb chops
- ¼ cup fresh mint leaves, chopped
- 2 tablespoons olive oil
- 2 tablespoons balsamic vinegar
- 2 cloves garlic, minced
- 1 tablespoon Dijon mustard
- Black pepper, and salt, to taste

Directions:

1. At 400°F (200°C), preheat your oven.
2. Season the lamb chops with black pepper, and salt on both sides.
3. Heat olive oil in an oven-safe skillet over medium-high heat. Add the lamb chops to the skillet and sear them for about 2-3 minutes per side until browned.
4. Transfer the skillet to the preheated oven and roast the lamb chops for about 10-12 minutes for medium-rare.
5. Remove the skillet from the oven and transfer the lamb chops to a plate. Cover them with foil and let them rest for a few minutes.
6. In the same skillet, heat balsamic vinegar over medium heat. Stir in the garlic mince and Dijon mustard. Cook for about 1 minute until the flavors meld together.
7. Remove the skillet from heat and stir in the chopped mint leaves.
8. Plate the lamb chops and drizzle the mint pan sauce over them.
9. Serve the lamb chops with mint pan sauce hot with your choice of side dishes. Enjoy!

Nutritional Information (per serving): Calories: 389; Fat: 33.2g; Sodium: 112mg; Carbs: 1.3g; Fibers: 0.6g; Sugar: 0.1g; Proteins: 19.5g

49. Chicken Kebabs

Prep time: 1 hr. 5 minutes. | **Cook time:** 10 minutes. | **Serves:** 2

Ingredients:

- 1.5 lbs. boneless chicken breasts, cut into bite-sized pieces
- ¼ cup plain yogurt
- 2 tablespoons olive oil
- 2 tablespoons lemon juice
- 2 cloves garlic, minced
- 1 teaspoon paprika
- 1 teaspoon (ground) cumin
- ½ teaspoon (ground) coriander
- ½ teaspoon (ground) turmeric
- ½ teaspoon salt
- ¼ teaspoon black pepper
- Wooden skewers, soaked in water for 30 minutes

Directions:

1. In a mixing bowl, mix the yogurt, olive oil, lemon juice, garlic mince, paprika, cumin, coriander, turmeric, salt, and black pepper. Mix well to create a marinade.
2. Add the chicken pieces to the marinade and toss until evenly covered. Cover the bowl with plastic wrap and refrigerate for at least 1 hour to enable the flavors to mingle.
3. Prepare your grill or grill pan to medium heat.
4. Thread the marinated chicken onto the moistened wooden skewers, allowing a tiny space between each piece.
5. Place the chicken skewers on the hot grill and cook for 8-10 minutes, rotating regularly, until the chicken is cooked through and browned on the edges.
6. Once cooked, remove the chicken kebabs from the grill and let them rest for a few minutes.
7. Serve the chicken kebabs hot with your choice of side dishes, like rice, salad, or pita bread.
8. Enjoy your flavorful and juicy chicken kebabs!

Nutritional Information (per serving): Calories: 461; Fat: 21.4g; Sodium: 608mg; Carbs: 4.3g; Fibers: 1.5g; Sugar: 1g; Proteins: 62.3g

50.Crunchy Chicken & Mango Salad

Prep time: 10 minutes. | **Cook time:** 10 minutes. | **Serves:** 4

Ingredients:

- For the salad:
- 2 boneless, skinless chicken breasts, cooked and shredded
- 2 cups mixed salad greens
- 1 ripe mango, peeled, pitted, and diced
- ½ cup cherry tomatoes, halved
- ¼ cup sliced red onion
- ¼ cup chopped fresh cilantro
- ¼ cup chopped cashews
- For the dressing:
- 2 tablespoons lime juice
- 2 tablespoons olive oil
- 1 tablespoon honey
- 1 teaspoon Dijon mustard
- Black pepper, and salt, as required

Directions:

1. In a suitable-sized salad bowl, combine shredded chicken, mixed salad greens, diced mango, cherry tomatoes, red onion, cilantro, and chopped cashews.
2. In a suitable-sized bowl, mix lime juice, olive oil, honey, Dijon mustard, black pepper, and salt to make the dressing.
3. Drizzle the prepared dressing over the salad and toss gently to coat all the ingredients.
4. Serve the crunchy chicken and mango salad as a refreshing and satisfying meal.

Nutritional Information (per serving): Calories: 328; Fat: 16.7g; Sodium: 97mg; Carbs: 23.6g; Fibers: 2.1g; Sugar: 17.1g; Proteins: 23.5g

51.Spicy Orange Beef & Broccoli Stir-Fry

Prep time: 15 minutes. | **Cook time:** 15 minutes. | **Serves:** 4

Ingredients:

- 1 lb. beef sirloin or flank steak, thinly sliced
- 4 cups broccoli florets
- 1 orange, zest and juice
- 2 tablespoons (low-sodium) soy sauce
- 2 tablespoons (low-sodium) hoisin sauce
- 2 tablespoons honey
- 1 tablespoon rice vinegar
- 1 tablespoon vegetable oil
- 2 cloves garlic, minced
- 1 teaspoon ginger, grated
- ½ teaspoon red pepper flakes
- Black pepper, and salt, to taste
- Sesame seeds, for garnish

Directions:

1. In a suitable-sized bowl, mix orange zest, orange juice, soy sauce, hoisin sauce, honey, rice vinegar, garlic mince, grated ginger, red pepper flakes, black pepper, and salt. Set aside.
2. Heat vegetable oil in a suitable-sized skillet or wok over high heat. Add the sliced beef and stir-fry for about 2-3 minutes until browned. Remove the beef from the skillet and set aside.
3. In the same skillet, add the broccoli florets. Stir-fry for about 4-5 minutes until crisp-tender.
4. Return the beef to the skillet with the broccoli. Pour the sauce mixture over the ingredients.
5. Continue stir-frying for another 2-3 minutes until the sauce thickens and coats the beef and broccoli. Season with black pepper and salt to taste.
6. Remove it from the heat and transfer the spicy orange beef and broccoli stir-fry to a serving dish.
7. Garnish with sesame seeds and serve hot over steamed rice or noodles. Enjoy!

Nutritional Information (per serving): Calories: 354; Fat: 11.2g; Sodium: 686mg; Carbs: 25.2g; Fibers: 3.9g; Sugar: 16.9g; Proteins: 38.3g

52.Pork & Kimchi Fried Rice

Prep time: 10 minutes. | **Cook time:** 15 minutes. | **Serves:** 4

Ingredients:

*   2 cups cooked white rice, chilled (preferably day-old)
*   1 cup cooked pork, diced
*   1 cup kimchi, chopped
*   ½ cup frozen peas and carrots
*   2 cloves garlic, minced
*   2 tablespoons vegetable oil
*   2 tablespoons (low-sodium) soy sauce
*   1 tablespoon sesame oil
*   2 green onions, chopped
*   2 eggs, beaten
*   Black pepper, and salt, to taste

Directions:

1. Heat vegetable oil in a suitable-sized skillet or wok over medium heat. Add the garlic mince and cook for about 1 minute until fragrant.
2. Toss in the diced pork and cook for another 2-3 minutes until heated through.
3. Stir in the chopped kimchi and frozen peas and carrots. Cook for about 3-4 minutes until the vegetables are tender.
4. Push the pork and kimchi mixture to one side of the skillet. Pour the beaten eggs into the other side of the skillet and scramble them.
5. Once the eggs are cooked, mix them with the pork and kimchi mixture.
6. Add the chilled cooked rice to the skillet. Drizzle soy sauce and sesame oil over the rice. Stir-fry everything for about 5-6 minutes until the rice is heated through and well-coated with the sauce.
7. Season with black pepper and salt to taste. Stir in the chopped green onions.
8. Remove it from the heat and transfer the pork and kimchi fried rice to a serving dish.
9. Serve the pork and kimchi fried rice hot. Enjoy!

Nutritional Information (per serving): Calories: 387; Fat: 15.6g; Sodium: 408mg; Carbs: 35.4g; Fibers: 1.8g; Sugar: 2.7g; Proteins: 32.7g

Fish & Seafood

53. Healthy Baked Halibut

Prep time: 15 minutes. | **Cook time:** 15 minutes. | Serves: 4

Ingredients:

- 8 oz halibut filets thawed
- 2 cups green beans
- 1 cup grape tomatoes
- 1 ½ tablespoons extra virgin olive oil
- ½ teaspoon Italian seasoning
- 1 lemon juice of
- Black pepper, and salt, as required

Directions:

1. At 350°F (180°C), preheat your oven.
2. Take a plate, put the fish on it, and use paper towels to pat it dry.
3. Prepare the tomatoes and green beans by slicing them, and then arrange them evenly in a 13-inch by 9-inch casserole dish. Place the halibut on top of the vegetables.
4. Drizzle the oil over the vegetables and fish, followed by the lemon juice. Sprinkle some salt, pepper, and Italian seasoning on top.
5. Bake for 15-18 minutes until the fish becomes opaque and easily flakes with a fork and the vegetables are cooked al dente.
6. Serve the dish immediately.

Nutritional Information (per serving): Calories: 234; Fat: 11.7g; Sodium: 66mg; Carbs: 11.5g; Fiber 4.8g; Sugars 4g; Protein 22.8g

54. Steamed Tilapia in Wine Sauce

Prep time: 10 minutes. | **Cook time:** 10 minutes. | Serves: 4

Ingredients:

- 4 tilapia fillets
- 1 cup dry white wine
- 2 tablespoons almond butter
- 2 cloves of garlic, minced
- 1 tablespoon fresh lemon juice
- 1 tablespoon chopped fresh parsley
- Black pepper, and salt, as required
- Lemon slices for garnish

Directions:

1. Rinse the tilapia fillets under cold water and pat them dry with paper towels.
2. In a suitable-sized skillet or saucepan, mix the white wine, butter, garlic mince, lemon juice, black pepper, and salt. Place the skillet over medium heat.
3. Once the liquid starts to simmer, place a steamer basket inside the skillet.
4. Arrange the tilapia fillets in a single layer in the steamer basket. Cover the skillet with a lid and let the fish steam for about 8-10 minutes.
5. Carefully remove the steamer basket from the skillet and transfer the tilapia fillets to a serving plate.
6. Drizzle the wine sauce from the skillet over the steamed tilapia fillets.
7. Sprinkle with chopped fresh parsley and garnish with lemon slices.
8. Serve the Steamed Tilapia in Wine Sauce with your choice of steamed vegetables, roasted potatoes, or crusty bread.

Nutritional Information (per serving): Calories: 104; Fat: 5.8g; Sodium: 46mg; Carbs: 2.2g; Fibers: 0.1g; Sugar: 0.6g; Proteins: 0.5g

55. Miso-Maple Salmon

Prep time: 30 minutes. | **Cook time:** 10 minutes. |
Serves: 4

Ingredients:

- 4 salmon fillets
- 2 tablespoons miso paste
- 2 tablespoons maple syrup
- 1 tablespoon (low-sodium) soy sauce
- 1 tablespoon rice vinegar
- 1 teaspoon grated ginger
- 2 cloves garlic, minced
- 1 tablespoon vegetable oil
- Sesame seeds, for garnish
- Sliced green onions, for garnish

Directions:

1. In a suitable-sized bowl, mix miso paste, maple syrup, soy sauce, rice vinegar, grated ginger, and garlic mince until well combined.
2. Place the salmon fillets in a shallow dish and pour the miso-maple marinade over them. Make sure the salmon is coated evenly. Let it marinate for 15-20 minutes.
3. Heat vegetable oil in a suitable-sized skillet over medium-high heat.
4. Remove the salmon from the marinade, allowing any excess marinade to drip off, and place the fillets skin-side down in the skillet.
5. Cook the salmon for about 4-5 minutes per side, until the fish is cooked through and nicely caramelized.
6. While cooking, you can baste the salmon with the remaining marinade to add extra flavor and glaze.
7. Once cooked, remove the salmon from the skillet and transfer to a serving plate.
8. Garnish with sesame seeds and sliced green onions.
9. Serve the miso-maple salmon with steamed rice or a side of your choice. Enjoy!

Nutritional Information (per serving): Calories: 317; Fat: 15g; Sodium: 626mg; Carbs: 10.1g; Fibers: 0.6g; Sugar: 6.6g; Proteins: 35.9g

56. Charred Shrimp & Pesto Buddha Bowls

Prep time: 10 minutes. | **Cook time:** 10 minutes. |
Serves: 2

Ingredients:

- For the shrimp:
- 1 lb. large shrimp, peeled and deveined
- 2 tablespoons olive oil
- 1 teaspoon smoked paprika
- ½ teaspoon garlic powder
- Black pepper, and salt, as required
- For the pesto:
- 2 cups fresh basil leaves
- ½ cup low-fat parmesan cheese, grated
- ¼ cup pine nuts
- 2 cloves garlic
- ¼ cup extra-virgin olive oil
- Black pepper, and salt, as required
- For the Buddha bowls:
- Cooked quinoa or rice
- Sliced cucumbers
- Cherry tomatoes, halved
- Sliced avocado
- Mixed greens or lettuce

Directions:

1. Preheat the grill or a grill pan over medium-high heat.
2. In a bowl, toss the shrimp with olive oil, smoked paprika, garlic powder, black pepper, and salt until coated.
3. Grill the shrimp for 2-3 minutes per side until they are pink and cooked through. Set aside.
4. In a food processor, combine basil leaves, Parmesan cheese, pine nuts, garlic, olive oil, black pepper, and salt. Process until smooth to make the pesto sauce.
5. Assemble the Buddha bowls by placing a scoop of cooked quinoa or rice in each bowl.
6. Arrange the grilled shrimp, sliced cucumbers, cherry tomatoes, sliced avocado, and mixed greens or lettuce in separate sections around the bowl.
7. Drizzle the pesto sauce over the top of each Buddha bowl.

Nutritional Information (per serving): Calories: 455; Fat: 27.4g; Sodium: 351mg; Carbs: 9.3g; Fibers: 1.5g; Sugar: 1g; Proteins: 48.3g

57. Roasted Salmon with Sautéed Balsamic Spinach

Prep time: 15 minutes. | **Cook time:** 20 minutes. | Serves: 4

Ingredients:

- **For the salmon:**
- 4 salmon fillets (6 oz.)
- 1 tablespoon olive oil
- 1 teaspoon paprika
- ½ teaspoon garlic powder
- ½ teaspoon dried thyme
- Black pepper, and salt, as required
- **For the sautéed balsamic spinach:**
- 2 tablespoons olive oil
- 2 cloves of garlic, minced
- 8 cups fresh spinach leaves
- 2 tablespoons balsamic vinegar
- Black pepper, and salt, as required

Directions:

1. For the salmon:
2. At 400°F (200°C), preheat your air fryer.
3. Rub the salmon fillets with olive oil and season them with paprika, garlic powder, dried thyme, black pepper, and salt. Make sure the fillets are evenly coated.
4. Place the seasoned salmon fillets in the air fryer basket, ensuring they are not overcrowded.
5. Cook the salmon in the air fryer for about 10-12 minutes.
6. Once cooked, remove the salmon fillets from the air fryer and set them aside.
7. For the sautéed balsamic spinach:
8. Heat olive oil in a suitable-sized skillet over medium heat.
9. Add the garlic mince and sauté for about 1 min.
10. Add the fresh spinach leaves to the skillet and toss them gently until they start to wilt.
11. Drizzle the balsamic vinegar over the spinach and continue cooking for an additional 2-3 minutes.
12. Season with black pepper and salt to taste.
13. Divide the sautéed balsamic spinach onto plates.
14. Place a roasted salmon fillet on top of the spinach. Garnish with herbs if desired and enjoy.

Nutritional Information (per serving): Calories: 371; Fat: 17.8 g; Sodium: 148mg; Carbs: 3.4g; Fibers: 1.6g; Sugar: 0.4g; Proteins: 46g

58. Crumb-Coated Red Snapper

Prep time: 10 minutes. | **Cook time:** 15 minutes. | Serves: 4

Ingredients:

- 4 red snapper fillets (6 oz.)
- 1 cup bread crumbs
- ½ cup low-fat parmesan cheese, grated
- 1 teaspoon dried oregano
- 1 teaspoon dried basil
- ½ teaspoon garlic powder
- ½ teaspoon paprika
- Black pepper, and salt, as required
- 2 eggs, beaten
- 2 tablespoons olive oil
- Lemon wedges for serving

Directions:

1. At 400°F (200°C), preheat your oven. Line a baking sheet with parchment paper.
2. In a shallow dish, mix the bread crumbs, grated Parmesan cheese, dried oregano, dried basil, garlic powder, paprika, black pepper, and salt. Mix well.
3. Dip each red snapper fillet into the beaten eggs, allowing any excess to drip off.
4. Coat the fillets evenly with the breadcrumb mixture, pressing gently to adhere.
5. Heat olive oil in a suitable-sized skillet over medium heat. Place the breaded red snapper fillets in the skillet and cook for about 2-3 minutes per side until golden brown.
6. Transfer the seared red snapper fillets to the prepared baking sheet.
7. Bake it in your preheated oven for about 10-12 minutes.
8. Serve the Crumb-Coated Red Snapper with lemon wedges and your choice of side dishes like roasted potatoes, steamed vegetables, or a fresh salad.

Nutritional Information (per serving): Calories: 430; Fat: 14.4g; Sodium: 358mg; Carbs: 20.4g; Fibers: 1.5g; Sugar: 2g; Proteins: 52.4g

59. Halibut Soft Tacos

Prep time: 15 minutes. | **Cook time:** 10 minutes. | **Serves:** 4

Ingredients:

- 4 halibut fillets (6 oz.)
- 1 teaspoon (ground) cumin
- 1 teaspoon chili powder
- ½ teaspoon garlic powder
- ½ teaspoon paprika
- Black pepper, and salt, as required
- 2 tablespoons olive oil
- 8 small soft taco tortillas
- Shredded lettuce
- Diced tomatoes
- Sliced avocado
- Chopped fresh cilantro
- Lime wedges for serving

Directions:

1. In a suitable-sized bowl, mix the ground cumin, chili powder, garlic powder, paprika, black pepper, and salt.
2. Rub the spice mixture evenly onto both sides of the halibut fillets.
3. Heat olive oil in a suitable-sized skillet over medium heat. Add the seasoned halibut fillets to the skillet.
4. Cook the halibut for about 3-4 minutes per side.
5. Remove the cooked halibut from the skillet and let it rest for a minute. Then, flake the fish into smaller pieces.
6. Warm the soft taco tortillas according to package instructions.
7. Assemble the tacos by placing some shredded lettuce on each tortilla, followed by the flaked halibut.
8. Top with tomatoes, avocado, and cilantro.
9. To add freshness and acidity, squeeze lime juice over the tacos.
10. Serve the Halibut Soft Tacos as a delicious and customizable meal, allowing your guests to add their preferred toppings and enjoy!

Nutritional Information (per serving): Calories: 584; Fat: 20g; Sodium: 664mg; Carbs: 29g; Fibers: 8.4g; Sugar: 2.2g; Proteins: 70.8g

60. Cajun Salmon with Greek Yogurt Remoulade

Prep time: 10 minutes. | **Cook time:** 10 minutes. | **Serves:** 4

Ingredients:

- For the Cajun seasoning:
- 1 tablespoon paprika
- 1 tablespoon garlic powder
- 1 tablespoon onion powder
- 1 tablespoon dried thyme
- 1 tablespoon dried oregano
- 1 teaspoon cayenne pepper
- 1 teaspoon salt
- 1 teaspoon black pepper
- For the salmon:
- 4 salmon fillets
- 2 tablespoons Cajun seasoning
- 2 tablespoons olive oil
- For the Greek yogurt remoulade:
- ½ cup Greek yogurt
- 2 tablespoons low-fat mayonnaise
- 2 tablespoons Dijon mustard
- 1 tablespoon capers, chopped
- 1 tablespoon chopped fresh dill
- 1 tablespoon lemon juice
- Black pepper, and salt, as required

Directions:

1. In a suitable-sized bowl, mix all the Cajun seasoning ingredients.
2. Rub the Cajun seasoning evenly on both sides of the salmon fillets.
3. Heat olive oil in a suitable-sized skillet over medium-high heat.
4. Add the salmon fillets to the skillet and cook for about 4-5 minutes per side.
5. Prepare the Greek yogurt remoulade by combining Greek yogurt, mayonnaise, Dijon mustard, capers, chopped dill, lemon juice, black pepper, and salt in a bowl. Mix well.
6. Once the salmon is cooked, remove it from the skillet and let it rest for a few minutes before serving it.

Nutritional Information (per serving): Calories: 322; Fat: 18.5g; Sodium: 738mg; Carbs: 5.6g; Fibers: 2g; Sugar: 1.4g; Proteins: 35.7g

61. Mediterranean Sole

Prep time: 10 minutes. | **Cook time:** 10 minutes. |
Serves: 4

Ingredients:

- 4 sole fillets
- ¼ cup whole-wheat flour
- 1 teaspoon dried oregano
- 1 teaspoon dried thyme
- ½ teaspoon garlic powder
- ½ teaspoon paprika
- Black pepper, and salt, as required
- 2 tablespoons olive oil
- 2 tablespoons lemon juice
- 2 tablespoons capers, drained
- 1 tablespoon chopped fresh parsley
- Lemon wedges for serving

Directions:

1. In a shallow dish, mix the whole-wheat flour, dried oregano, dried thyme, garlic powder, paprika, black pepper, and salt.
2. Dredge each sole fillet in the flour mixture, shaking off any excess.
3. Heat olive oil in a suitable-sized skillet over medium heat. Add the floured sole fillets to the skillet.
4. Cook the sole fillets for about 2-3 minutes per side until lightly golden and cooked through.
5. Once cooked, remove the sole fillets from the skillet and transfer them to a serving dish.
6. In the same skillet, add lemon juice and capers. Cook for a minute, scraping the bottom of the skillet to incorporate any browned bits.
7. Pour the lemon-caper sauce over the cooked sole fillets.
8. Sprinkle with chopped fresh parsley and garnish with lemon wedges.
9. Serve the Mediterranean Sole with a side of roasted vegetables, couscous, or a salad for a light and flavorful meal.

Nutritional Information (per serving): Calories: 244; Fat: 9.2g; Sodium: 263mg; Carbs: 7.2g; Fibers: 0.8g; Sugar: 0.4g; Proteins: 31.8g

62. Tilapia & Lemon Sauce

Prep time: 15 minutes. | **Cook time:** 10 minutes. |
Serves: 4

Ingredients:

- 4 tilapia fillets
- ¼ cup whole-wheat flour
- Black pepper, and salt, as required
- 2 tablespoons almond butter
- 2 cloves of garlic, minced
- ½ cup (low-sodium) chicken broth
- Juice of 1 lemon
- 1 tablespoon chopped fresh parsley
- Lemon slices for garnish

Directions:

1. Rinse the tilapia fillets under cold water and pat them dry with paper towels.
2. Season the tilapia fillets with black pepper, and salt. Dredge them in the whole-wheat flour, shaking off any excess.
3. In a suitable-sized skillet, melt the butter over medium heat. Add the garlic mince and cook for about 1 minute until fragrant.
4. Place the floured tilapia fillets in the skillet and cook for about 3-4 minutes per side until golden brown and cooked through.
5. Remove the cooked tilapia fillets from the skillet and set them aside.
6. In the same skillet, add the chicken broth and lemon juice. Mix well, scraping the bottom of the skillet to incorporate any browned bits.
7. Cook the sauce for a couple of minutes until it slightly thickens.
8. Return the cooked tilapia fillets to the skillet and coat them with the lemon sauce.
9. Sprinkle with chopped fresh parsley and garnish with lemon slices.
10. Serve the Tilapia & Lemon Sauce with steamed vegetables, rice pilaf, or roasted potatoes.

Nutritional Information (per serving): Calories: 227; Fat: 8g; Sodium: 197mg; Carbs: 6.7g; Fibers: 0.3g; Sugar: 0.1g; Proteins: 33.6g

63. Martha's Fish Tacos

Prep time: 10 minutes. | **Cook time:** 15 minutes. |
Serves: 4

Ingredients:

- 1 lb. white fish fillets (cod or halibut)
- ½ cup whole-wheat flour
- 1 teaspoon chili powder
- ½ teaspoon garlic powder
- ½ teaspoon paprika
- Black pepper, and salt, as required
- Vegetable oil for frying
- 8 small soft taco tortillas
- Shredded lettuce
- Diced tomatoes
- Sliced avocado
- Sliced jalapeños
- Cilantro-lime crema (see recipe below)
- For the cilantro-lime crema:
- ½ cup low-fat sour cream
- ¼ cup chopped fresh cilantro
- Juice of 1 lime
- Salt to taste

Directions:

1. In a shallow dish, mix the whole-wheat flour, chili powder, garlic powder, paprika, black pepper, and salt.
2. Cut the white fish fillets into smaller pieces, if needed, to fit in the tortillas.
3. Dredge the fish pieces in the flour mixture, shaking off any excess.
4. Heat vegetable oil in a suitable-sized skillet over medium-high heat. Add the coated fish pieces and cook for about 3-4 minutes per side until golden brown and cooked through.
5. Remove the cooked fish from the skillet and let them drain on a paper towel-lined plate.
6. To make the cilantro-lime crema, mix the sour cream, chopped cilantro, lime juice, and salt in a bowl. Mix well.
7. Warm the soft taco tortillas according to package instructions.
8. Assemble the fish tacos by placing some shredded lettuce on each tortilla, followed by a piece of cooked fish.
9. Top with diced tomatoes, sliced avocado, sliced jalapeños (if desired), and a drizzle of cilantro-lime crema.
10. Serve Martha's Fish Tacos with a side of Mexican rice, black beans, or a refreshing salsa.

Nutritional Information (per serving): Calories: 456; Fat: 14.8g; Sodium: 581mg; Carbs: 40.7g; Fibers: 8.8g; Sugar: 2.2g; Proteins: 39.5g

64. Cedar Plank Salmon with Blackberry Sauce

Prep time: 10 minutes. | **Cook time:** 25 minutes. |
Serves: 4

Ingredients:

- 4 salmon fillets (6 oz.)
- Cedar planks for grilling (soaked in water for at least 1 hour)
- Black pepper, and salt, as required
- ¼ cup maple syrup
- 2 tablespoons (low-sodium) soy sauce
- 1 tablespoon Dijon mustard
- 1 cup fresh blackberries
- 1 tablespoon balsamic vinegar
- 1 tablespoon honey
- Fresh mint leaves for garnish

Directions:

1. Preheat your grill to medium-high heat.
2. Season the salmon fillets with black pepper, and salt.
3. Place the soaked cedar planks on the grill grates and close its lid. Allow the planks to heat up for a few minutes until they start to smoke slightly.
4. Place the seasoned salmon fillets directly onto the cedar planks. Close its lid and grill for about 12-15 minutes.
5. Meanwhile, prepare the blackberry sauce. In a small saucepan, mix the maple syrup, soy sauce, Dijon mustard, blackberries, balsamic vinegar, and honey.
6. Place the saucepan over medium heat and Cook the mixture to a simmer. Cook for about 5-7 minutes, stir occasionally, until the blackberries soften and release their juices.
7. Remove the blackberry sauce from the heat and let it cool slightly. Use a blender or immersion blender to blend the sauce until smooth. If desired, strain the sauce through a fine-mesh sieve to remove any seeds.

8. Once the salmon is cooked, remove the cedar planks from the grill. Transfer the grilled salmon fillets to a serving platter.
9. Drizzle the cedar plank salmon with the blackberry sauce.
10. Garnish with mint leaves and serve with a side of grilled vegetables, quinoa, or roasted potatoes. Enjoy the Cedar Plank Salmon with Blackberry Sauce!

Nutritional Information (per serving): Calories: 326; Fat: 11.4g; Sodium: 576mg; Carbs: 21.9g; Fibers: 2.1g; Sugar: 18g; Proteins: 35.7g

65. Grilled Mahi-mahi

Prep time: 40 minutes.| **Cook time:** 10 minutes.| **Serves:** 4

Ingredients:

- 4 mahi-mahi fillets (6 oz.)
- 2 tablespoons olive oil
- Juice of 1 lemon
- 2 cloves of garlic, minced
- 1 teaspoon paprika
- ½ teaspoon dried oregano
- Black pepper, and salt, as required
- Lemon wedges for serving

Directions:

1. Preheat your grill to medium-high heat.
2. In a suitable-sized bowl, mix the olive oil, lemon juice, garlic mince, paprika, dried oregano, black pepper, and salt.
3. Place the mahi-mahi fillets in a shallow dish and pour the marinade over them. Make sure the fillets are evenly coated. Allow them to marinate for about 20-30 minutes.
4. Remove the mahi-mahi fillets from the marinade and discard the remaining marinade.
5. Grill the mahi-mahi fillets on the preheated grill for about 4-5 minutes per side.
6. Remove the grilled mahi-mahi from the grill and let it rest for a few minutes.
7. Serve the Grilled Mahi-mahi with lemon wedges on the side. Pair it with a side of grilled vegetables, rice pilaf, or a fresh salad.

Nutritional Information (per serving): Calories: 242; Fat: 8.9g; Sodium: 256mg; Carbs: 0.9g; Fibers: 0.3g; Sugar: 0.1g; Proteins: 38g

66. Red Pepper & Parmesan Tilapia

Prep time: 10 minutes.| **Cook time:** 15 minutes.| **Serves:** 4

Ingredients:

- 4 tilapia fillets
- Black pepper, and salt, as required
- ½ cup low-fat parmesan cheese, grated
- ¼ cup bread crumbs
- ¼ cup finely chopped roasted red peppers
- 2 tablespoons melted almond butter
- Lemon wedges for serving

Directions:

1. At 400°F (200°C), preheat your oven. Line a baking sheet with parchment paper.
2. Season the tilapia fillets with black pepper, and salt, as required.
3. In a shallow dish, mix the grated Parmesan cheese, bread crumbs, and chopped roasted red peppers.
4. Dip each tilapia fillet into the melted butter, allowing any excess to drip off.
5. Coat the fillets evenly with the Parmesan and red pepper mixture, pressing gently to adhere.
6. Place the coated tilapia fillets on the prepared baking sheet.
7. Bake it in your preheated oven for about 12-15 minutes.
8. Remove the baked tilapia from the oven and let it rest for a minute.
9. Serve the Red Pepper & Parmesan Tilapia with lemon wedges for squeezing over the fish. Pair it with steamed vegetables, quinoa, or a side of your choice.

Nutritional Information (per serving): Calories: 232; Fat: 8.9g; Sodium: 210mg; Carbs: 5.7g; Fibers: 0.5g; Sugar: 0.9g; Proteins: 34.2g

67. Chimichurri Baked Flounder

Prep time: 10 minutes. | **Cook time:** 15 minutes. | **Serves:** 4

Ingredients:

- 4 flounder fillets
- Black pepper, and salt, as required
- 1 cup fresh parsley leaves
- ¼ cup fresh cilantro leaves
- 3 cloves of garlic
- 2 tablespoons red wine vinegar
- ¼ cup olive oil
- ¼ teaspoon red pepper flakes
- Lemon wedges for serving

Directions:

1. At 400°F (200°C), preheat your oven. Line a baking sheet with parchment paper.
2. Season the flounder fillets with black pepper, and salt, as required.
3. In a food processor or blender, mix the fresh parsley leaves, fresh cilantro leaves, garlic cloves, red wine vinegar, olive oil, black pepper, and salt. Blend until you achieve a smooth chimichurri sauce. If desired, add red pepper flakes for a bit of heat.
4. Place the flounder fillets on the prepared baking sheet.
5. Spoon a generous amount of the chimichurri sauce over each fillet, spreading it evenly.
6. Bake it in your preheated oven for about 10-12 minutes.
7. Remove the baked flounder from the oven and let it rest for a minute.
8. Serve the Chimichurri Baked Flounder with lemon wedges for squeezing over the fish. Pair it with roasted potatoes, steamed rice, or a side salad for a delicious and vibrant meal.

Nutritional Information (per serving): Calories: 267; Fat: 14.7g; Sodium: 143mg; Carbs: 1.8g; Fibers: 0.6g; Sugar: 0.2g; Proteins: 31.3g

68. Grilled Halibut with Blueberry Salsa

Prep time: 10 minutes. | **Cook time:** 10 minutes. | **Serves:** 4

Ingredients:

- 4 halibut fillets (6 oz.)
- Black pepper, and salt, as required
- 2 tablespoons olive oil
- For the blueberry salsa:
- 1 cup fresh blueberries
- ¼ cup diced red onion
- 1 jalapeño pepper, seeded and finely chopped
- Juice of 1 lime
- 2 tablespoons chopped fresh cilantro
- Salt to taste

Directions:

1. Preheat your grill to medium-high heat.
2. Season the halibut fillets with black pepper, and salt, as required.
3. Brush both sides of the halibut fillets with olive oil.
4. In a suitable-sized bowl, mix the fresh blueberries, diced red onion, jalapeño pepper, lime juice, chopped cilantro, and salt. Mix well to make the blueberry salsa.
5. Place the halibut fillets on the preheated grill and cook for about 4-5 minutes per side.
6. Remove the grilled halibut from the grill and let it rest for a few minutes.
7. Serve the Grilled Halibut with Blueberry Salsa on top of each fillet. Spoon the blueberry salsa generously over the fish.
8. Pair the dish with a side of grilled vegetables, quinoa, or roasted potatoes for a complete and flavorful meal.

Nutritional Information (per serving): Calories: 403; Fat: 13.9g; Sodium: 157mg; Carbs: 6.2g; Fibers: 1.2g; Sugar: 4g; Proteins: 60.9g

69. Walnut and Oat-Crusted Salmon

Prep time: 10 minutes. | **Cook time:** 15 minutes. | **Serves:** 4

Ingredients:

- 4 salmon fillets (6 oz.)
- Black pepper, and salt, as required
- ½ cup walnuts
- ½ cup rolled oats
- 2 tablespoons Dijon mustard
- 2 tablespoons honey
- 1 tablespoon olive oil

Directions:

1. At 400°F (200°C), preheat your oven. Line a baking sheet with parchment paper.
2. Season the salmon fillets with black pepper, and salt, as required.
3. In a food processor, pulse the walnuts and rolled oats until they are coarsely ground.
4. In a suitable-sized bowl, mix the Dijon mustard and honey.
5. Brush the top side of each salmon fillet with the Dijon mustard-honey mixture.
6. Press the walnut and oat mixture onto the mustard-honey-coated side of each fillet, creating a crust.
7. Heat olive oil in an oven-safe skillet over medium heat. Once hot, add the salmon fillets, crust side down, and cook for about 2-3 minutes until the crust is golden brown.
8. Transfer the skillet to the preheated oven and bake for about 10-12 minutes.
9. Remove the Walnut and Oat-Crusted Salmon from the oven and let it rest for a minute.
10. Serve the salmon fillets with your choice of side dishes like roasted vegetables, couscous, or a fresh salad.

Nutritional Information (per serving): Calories: 438; Fat: 24.7g; Sodium: 168mg; Carbs: 17.6g; Fibers: 2.4g; Sugar: 9g; Proteins: 40g

70. Grilled Blackened Shrimp Tacos

Prep time: 10 minutes. | **Cook time:** 20 minutes. | **Serves:** 4

Ingredients:

- **For the blackened seasoning:**
- 1 tablespoon paprika
- 1 teaspoon garlic powder
- 1 teaspoon onion powder
- 1 teaspoon dried thyme
- 1 teaspoon dried oregano
- 1 teaspoon cayenne pepper
- 1 teaspoon smoked paprika
- ½ teaspoon salt
- ½ teaspoon black pepper
- For the shrimp:
- 1 lb. large shrimp, peeled and deveined
- 2 tablespoons blackened seasoning
- 2 tablespoons olive oil
- **For the tacos:**
- 8 small corn tortillas
- Shredded lettuce
- Diced tomatoes
- Sliced avocado
- Lime wedges
- Cilantro, chopped

Directions:

1. In a suitable-sized bowl, mix all the blackened seasoning ingredients.
2. Pat the shrimp dry with paper towels and place them in a bowl.
3. Sprinkle the blackened seasoning over the shrimp and toss to coat them evenly.
4. Heat olive oil in a grill pan or skillet over medium-high heat.
5. Add the seasoned shrimp to the pan and cook for 2-3 minutes per side.
6. Warm the corn tortillas in a dry skillet or on a grill.
7. To assemble the tacos, place a few shrimps on each tortilla.
8. Top with shredded lettuce, diced tomatoes, sliced avocado, and a squeeze of lime juice.
9. Sprinkle with chopped cilantro if desired.
10. Serve it immediately. Enjoy!

Nutritional Information (per serving): Calories: 269; Fat: 8.8g; Sodium: 456mg; Carbs: 26.2g; Fibers: 4.2g; Sugar: 1.1g; Proteins: 24.6g

71.Green Curry Salmon with Green Beans

Prep time: 10 minutes. | **Cook time:** 25 minutes. |
Serves: 4

Ingredients:

- 4 salmon fillets (6 oz.)
- Black pepper, and salt, as required
- 1 tablespoon olive oil
- 1 tablespoon green curry paste
- 1 can (13.5 oz.) coconut milk
- 1 tablespoon fish sauce
- 1 tablespoon lime juice
- 1 cup fresh or frozen green beans
- Fresh cilantro leaves for garnish
- Cooked rice for serving

Directions:

1. Season the salmon fillets with black pepper, and salt, as required.
2. Heat olive oil in a suitable-sized skillet over medium heat. Add the salmon fillets, skin side down, and cook for about 4-5 minutes until the skin is crispy and the salmon is lightly browned. Flip the fillets and cook for an additional 2-3 minutes on the other side. Remove the salmon fillets from the skillet and set them aside.
3. In the same skillet, add the green curry paste and cook for about 1 minute, stirring constantly to release its flavors.
4. Pour in the coconut milk, fish sauce, and lime juice. Mix well to mix the ingredients.
5. Add the green beans to the skillet and simmer for about 5 minutes.
6. Return the salmon fillets to the skillet, nestling them into the curry sauce.
7. Cook for another 2-3 minutes, allowing the salmon to absorb some of the flavors from the curry sauce.
8. Garnish the Green Curry Salmon with fresh cilantro leaves.
9. Serve the salmon over cooked rice, spooning the green curry sauce and green beans on top. Enjoy this delicious and aromatic dish!

Nutritional Information (per serving): Calories: 405; Fat: 28.1g; Sodium: 585mg; Carbs: 5g; Fibers: 1g; Sugar: 0.6g; Proteins: 36.5g

Vegetarian and Vegan Dishes

72. Lentil & Vegetable Soup with Parmesan

Prep time: 10 minutes. | **Cook time:** 35 minutes. | **Serves:** 4

Ingredients:

- 1 cup dried lentils, rinsed
- 1 tablespoon olive oil
- 1 onion, diced
- 2 carrots, diced
- 2 celery stalks, diced
- 3 cloves of garlic, minced
- 1 teaspoon dried thyme
- 1 teaspoon dried oregano
- 1 can (14.5 oz.) diced tomatoes
- 4 cups (low-sodium) vegetable broth
- Black pepper, and salt, as required
- Low-fat parmesan cheese, grated for serving
- Fresh parsley for garnish

Directions:

1. In a suitable-sized pot, heat up the olive oil over medium heat. Toss in the diced onion, carrots, celery, and garlic mince. Sauté for about 5 minutes.
2. Add the dried lentils, dried thyme, dried oregano, diced tomatoes (with their juices), and vegetable broth to the pot. Mix well to combine.
3. Cook the mixture to a boil, then reduce its heat to low. Cover the pot and simmer for about 25-30 minutes.
4. Season the soup with black pepper, and salt, as required.
5. Divide the Lentil & Vegetable Soup into bowls. Top each serving with grated Parmesan cheese and fresh parsley.
6. Serve the soup hot and enjoy its comforting flavors and hearty texture.

Nutritional Information (per serving): Calories: 276; Fat: 5.6g; Sodium: 298mg ; Carbs: 38.5g; Fibers: 17g; Sugar: 5.7g; Proteins: 18.4g

73. Sweet Potato & Bean Enchiladas

Prep time: 10 minutes. | **Cook time:** 30 minutes. | **Serves:** 4

Ingredients:

- 2 medium sweet potatoes, peeled and diced
- 1 tablespoon olive oil
- 1 onion, diced
- 2 cloves of garlic, minced
- 1 can (15 oz.) black beans, rinsed and drained
- 1 can (10 oz.) enchilada sauce
- 1 teaspoon (ground) cumin
- 1 teaspoon chili powder
- Black pepper, and salt, as required
- 8 small flour tortillas
- 1 cup shredded low-fat cheddar cheese
- Fresh cilantro for garnish

Directions:

1. At 375°F (190°C), preheat your oven. Grease a baking dish with cooking spray.
2. Place the diced sweet potatoes in a microwave-safe bowl. Microwave them for about 5 minutes.
3. In a suitable-sized skillet, heat up the olive oil over medium heat. Toss in the diced onion and garlic mince. Sauté for about 5 minutes.
4. Add the cooked sweet potatoes, black beans, enchilada sauce, ground cumin, chili powder, black pepper, and salt to the skillet. Mix well to combine and cook for another 2-3 minutes to heat everything through.
5. Spoon the sweet potato and bean mixture onto each flour tortilla, roll them up, and place them seam-side down in the greased baking dish.
6. Sprinkle the shredded cheddar cheese over the enchiladas.
7. Bake them in your preheated oven for about 15 minutes.
8. Remove the enchiladas from the oven and let them cool for a few minutes.
9. Garnish Sweet Potato & Bean Enchiladas with fresh cilantro before serving. Enjoy this quick and flavorful vegetarian dish!

Nutritional Information (per serving): Calories: 389; Fat: 14.5g; Sodium: 392mg; Carbs: 39.2g; Fibers: 12.5g; Sugar: 11.2g; Proteins: 14.7g

74. Crispy Egg Noodles with Tofu & Peanut Sauce

Prep time: 10 minutes. | **Cook time:** 20 minutes. | **Serves:** 4

Ingredients:

- 8 oz. egg noodles
- 2 tablespoons vegetable oil
- 1 block (14 oz.) firm tofu, drained and cubed
- Black pepper, and salt, as required
- 1 red bell pepper, sliced
- 2 cups shredded cabbage
- ¼ cup creamy peanut butter
- 2 tablespoons (low-sodium) soy sauce
- 1 tablespoon lime juice
- 1 tablespoon honey
- 1 teaspoon sesame oil
- ¼ teaspoon red pepper flakes
- Chopped peanuts and sliced green onions for garnish

Directions:

1. Cook the egg noodles as per package instructions. Drain and set them aside.
2. In a suitable-sized skillet, heat up the vegetable oil over medium heat. Add the cubed tofu, season with black pepper, and salt, and cook until it turns golden brown on all sides. Remove the tofu from the skillet and set it aside.
3. In the same skillet, add the sliced red bell pepper and shredded cabbage. Sauté for about 3-4 minutes.
4. In a suitable-sized bowl, mix the peanut butter, soy sauce, lime juice, honey, sesame oil, and red pepper flakes to make the peanut sauce.
5. Push the vegetables to one side of the skillet and pour the peanut sauce into the empty space. Heat it for a minute, stirring continuously to warm it through.
6. Add the cooked egg noodles and crispy tofu to the skillet. Toss everything until the noodles and tofu are coated with the peanut sauce and heated through.

7. Remove the skillet from the heat.
8. Garnish the Crispy Egg Noodles with Tofu & Peanut Sauce with chopped peanuts and sliced green onions.
9. Serve the dish hot and enjoy the delightful combination of crispy noodles, tender tofu, and flavorful peanut sauce.

Nutritional Information (per serving): Calories: 304; Fat: 18.7g; Sodium: 539mg; Carbs: 27.3g; Fibers: 3.3g; Sugar: 9g; Proteins: 10.5g

75. Seitan BBQ Sandwiches

Prep time: 15 minutes. | **Cook time:** 1 hr. 10 minutes. | **Serves:** 4

Ingredients:

- **For the seitan:**
- 1 cup vital wheat gluten
- ¼ cup nutritional yeast
- 1 teaspoon smoked paprika
- 1 teaspoon garlic powder
- 1 teaspoon onion powder
- ½ teaspoon salt
- ½ teaspoon black pepper
- 1 cup (low-sodium) vegetable broth
- 2 tablespoons (low-sodium) soy sauce
- 2 tablespoons tomato paste
- **For the BBQ sauce:**
- 1 cup ketchup
- 2 tablespoons apple cider vinegar
- 2 tablespoons maple syrup
- 1 tablespoon Dijon mustard
- 1 tablespoon Worcestershire sauce
- 1 teaspoon smoked paprika
- ½ teaspoon garlic powder
- ½ teaspoon onion powder
- black pepper, and salt, as required
- For the sandwiches:
- 4 hamburger buns
- Sliced pickles
- Sliced red onions
- Coleslaw

Directions:

1. At 350°F (175°C), preheat your oven.

2. In a mixing bowl, combine vital wheat gluten, nutritional yeast, smoked paprika, garlic powder, onion powder, salt, and black pepper.
3. In a separate bowl, mix vegetable broth, soy sauce, and tomato paste.
4. Stir in the dry flour mixture and stir until a dough forms.
5. Knead the dough for a few minutes until it becomes elastic.
6. Shape the dough into a log and wrap it tightly in aluminum foil.
7. Bake the wrapped seitan in your preheated oven for 1 hour.
8. While the seitan is baking, prepare the BBQ sauce by mixing ketchup, apple cider vinegar, maple syrup, Dijon mustard, Worcestershire sauce, smoked paprika, garlic powder, onion powder, black pepper, and salt in a small saucepan. Heat over medium heat, stir occasionally, until heated through.
9. Remove the baked seitan from the oven and let it cool slightly. Slice the seitan into thin strips after removing the wrapper.
10. Heat a skillet over medium-high heat and add the sliced seitan.
11. Pour the BBQ sauce over the seitan and cook for 5-7 minutes, stir occasionally, until the seitan is coated and heated through.
12. Toast the hamburger buns if desired. Place a generous amount of BBQ seitan on each bun.
13. Add sliced pickles, sliced red onions, and coleslaw if desired.
14. Serve the seitan BBQ sandwiches hot and enjoy!

Nutritional Information (per serving): Calories: 335; Fat: 3.5g; Sodium: 513mg; Carbs: 55.5g; Fibers: 4.5g; Sugar: 24.8g; Proteins: 23.8g

76.Zucchini-Chickpea Veggie Burgers with Tahini-Ranch Sauce

Prep time: 10 minutes. | **Cook time:** 15 minutes. | **Serves:** 4

Ingredients:

- For the veggie burgers:
- 2 cups grated zucchini
- 1 can (15 oz.) chickpeas, drained and rinsed
- ½ cup breadcrumbs
- ¼ cup finely chopped onion
- 2 cloves garlic, minced
- 2 tablespoons chopped fresh parsley
- 1 teaspoon (ground) cumin
- ½ teaspoon salt
- ¼ teaspoon black pepper
- 2 tablespoons olive oil, for cooking
- For the tahini-ranch sauce:
- ¼ cup tahini
- ¼ cup plain Greek yogurt
- 1 tablespoon lemon juice
- 1 tablespoon chopped fresh dill
- 1 tablespoon chopped fresh chives
- 1 clove garlic, minced
- Black pepper, and salt, as required
- For serving:
- Burger buns
- Lettuce leaves
- Sliced tomatoes
- Sliced red onions

Directions:

1. In a suitable-sized bowl, combine grated zucchini, chickpeas, breadcrumbs, onion, garlic, parsley, cumin, salt, and black pepper. Mix well until everything is evenly combined.
2. Using your hands, shape the mixture into patties, about ½-inch thick and 3 inches in diameter. Put them on a parchment-lined baking pan.
3. Heat olive oil in a suitable-sized skillet over medium heat.
4. Cook the veggie burgers for about 4-5 minutes per side.
5. While the burgers are cooking, prepare the tahini-ranch sauce. In a suitable-sized bowl, mix tahini, Greek yogurt, lemon juice, dill, chives, garlic, black pepper, and salt until smooth and creamy.
6. Once the veggie burgers are cooked, remove them from the skillet and let them cool slightly.
7. Toast the burger buns if desired and assemble the burgers. Spread a generous amount of tahini-ranch sauce on the bottom bun, then add a veggie burger patty, lettuce leaves, sliced tomatoes, and sliced red.

Nutritional Information (per serving): Calories: 300; Fat: 17.4g; Sodium: 426mg; Carbs: 28.7g; Fibers: 6.2g; Sugar: 4.7g; Proteins: 10.7g

77. Lemon-Pepper Linguine with Squash

Prep time: 10 minutes. | **Cook time:** 10 minutes. | **Serves:** 4

Ingredients:

- 8 oz. linguine pasta
- 2 tablespoons olive oil
- 2 cloves of garlic, minced
- 1 small yellow squash, thinly sliced
- 1 small zucchini, thinly sliced
- Zest and juice of 1 lemon
- 1 teaspoon lemon pepper seasoning
- Black pepper, and salt, as required
- Low-fat parmesan cheese, grated for serving
- Fresh basil leaves for garnish

Directions:

1. Cook the linguine pasta as per package instructions. Drain once cooked then set it aside.
2. In a suitable-sized skillet, heat up the olive oil over medium heat. Add the minced garlic and cook until fragrant, about 1 minute.
3. Add the sliced yellow squash and zucchini to the skillet. Sauté for about 5-6 minutes.
4. Add the cooked linguine to the skillet and toss everything together.
5. Sprinkle the lemon zest, lemon juice, and lemon pepper seasoning over the pasta and vegetables. As needed, season with black pepper and salt. Toss again to coat everything evenly.
6. Remove the skillet from the heat.
7. Serve the Lemon-Pepper Linguine with Squash in bowls. Garnish with basil leaves and grated Parmesan cheese on top.
8. Enjoy this light and refreshing pasta dish with a burst of lemony flavor.

Nutritional Information (per serving): Calories: 313; Fat: 8.1g; Sodium: 8mg; Carbs: 50g; Fibers: 2.9g; Sugar: 2g; Proteins: 10.7g

78. Mushroom Shawarma with Yogurt-Tahini Sauce

Prep time: 10 minutes. | **Cook time:** 10 minutes. | **Serves:** 4

Ingredients:

- 8 oz. mushrooms, sliced
- 1 tablespoon olive oil
- 1 teaspoon (ground) cumin
- 1 teaspoon (ground) coriander
- ½ teaspoon (ground) paprika
- ¼ teaspoon (ground) turmeric
- Black pepper, and salt, as required
- 4 pita breads
- 1 cup plain Greek yogurt
- 2 tablespoons tahini
- 1 tablespoon lemon juice
- 2 cloves of garlic, minced
- Chopped fresh parsley for garnish
- Sliced cucumbers and tomatoes for serving

Directions:

1. In a suitable-sized skillet, heat up the olive oil over medium heat. Sauté the sliced mushrooms for around 5 minutes.
2. In a suitable-sized bowl, mix the ground cumin, ground coriander, ground paprika, ground turmeric, black pepper, and salt. Sprinkle this spice mixture over the mushrooms in the skillet. Mix well to coat the mushrooms evenly. Sauté for another 2-3 minutes to enable the flavors to mingle.
3. In a separate bowl, mix the Greek yogurt, tahini, lemon juice, and garlic mince to make the yogurt-tahini sauce. Mix well to incorporate all the ingredients.
4. Heat up the pita breads in a toaster or oven until warm and pliable.
5. Spread a generous amount of the yogurt-tahini sauce on each warm pita bread.
6. Divide the seasoned mushrooms among the pitas, placing them on top of the sauce.
7. Garnish the Mushroom Shawarma with chopped fresh parsley.
8. Serve the shawarma with sliced cucumbers and tomatoes on the side for a refreshing crunch.
9. Roll up the pitas and enjoy this flavorful and vegetarian twist on classic shawarma.

Nutritional Information (per serving): Calories: 281; Fat: 8.6g; Sodium: 353mg; Carbs: 38.7g; Fibers: 2.8g; Sugar: 3.2g; Proteins: 13.2g

79. Grain Bowl with Chickpeas & Cauliflower

Prep time: 10 minutes. | **Cook time:** 15 minutes. | **Serves:** 4

Ingredients:

- 1 cup cooked grains (quinoa, brown rice, or farro)
- 1 tablespoon olive oil
- 1 small head cauliflower, cut into florets
- 1 can (15 oz.) chickpeas, rinsed and drained
- 1 teaspoon (ground) cumin
- ½ teaspoon (ground) paprika
- Black pepper, and salt, as required
- 1 cup baby spinach or mixed greens
- ¼ cup crumbled feta cheese
- Lemon wedges for serving

Directions:

1. If the grains are not cooked yet, prepare them as per package instructions. Set aside.
2. In a suitable-sized skillet, heat up the olive oil over medium heat. Add the cauliflower florets and sauté for about 5 minutes.
3. Add the chickpeas to the skillet, along with the ground cumin, ground paprika, black pepper, and salt. Mix well to coat the cauliflower and chickpeas with the spices. Sauté for another 2-3 minutes to thoroughly cook everything.
4. Arrange the cooked grains in a serving bowl. Top with the sautéed cauliflower and chickpeas.
5. Add the baby spinach or mixed greens to the bowl.
6. Sprinkle the crumbled feta cheese over the grain bowl.
7. Serve the Grain Bowl with Chickpeas & Cauliflower with lemon wedges on the side for squeezing over the bowl.
8. Mix all the ingredients before eating, and enjoy this wholesome and nourishing grain bowl.

Nutritional Information (per serving): Calories: 350; Fat: 9.8g; Sodium: 180mg; Carbs: 53.2g; Fibers: 12.4g; Sugar: 7.9g; Proteins: 16.3g

80. Roasted Vegetable Bowls with Pesto

Prep time: 10 minutes. | **Cook time:** 25 minutes. | **Serves:** 4

Ingredients:

- 2 cups mixed vegetables (bell peppers, zucchini, eggplant, and cherry tomatoes), chopped
- 2 tablespoons olive oil
- Black pepper, and salt, as required
- 1 cup cooked quinoa or rice
- ¼ cup pesto sauce
- ¼ cup toasted pine nuts
- Fresh basil leaves for garnish

Directions:

1. At 400°F (200°C), preheat your oven.
2. In a suitable-sized baking sheet, toss the mixed vegetables with olive oil, black pepper, and salt.
3. Spread the vegetables out in a single layer on the baking sheet.
4. Roast for 20-25 minutes in a preheated oven.
5. In serving bowls, divide the cooked quinoa or rice.
6. Top the grains with the roasted vegetables.
7. Drizzle each bowl with pesto sauce.
8. Sprinkle toasted pine nuts over the bowls.
9. Garnish with basil leaves.
10. Serve the Roasted Vegetable Bowls with Pesto as a delicious and nutritious meal.

Nutritional Information (per serving): Calories: 398; Fat: 19.9g; Sodium: 372mg; Carbs: 47.8g; Fibers: 5.8g; Sugar: 1.4g; Proteins: 7.7g

81. Stuffed Sweet Potato with Hummus Dressing

Prep time: 10 minutes. | **Cook time:** 10 minutes. | Serves: 2

Ingredients:

- 2 medium-sized sweet potatoes
- 1 tablespoon olive oil
- Black pepper, and salt, as required
- 1 can (15 oz.) chickpeas, rinsed and drained
- 1 teaspoon (ground) cumin
- ½ teaspoon smoked paprika
- ¼ cup chopped fresh parsley
- ¼ cup hummus
- Juice of ½ lemon
- Chopped green onions for garnish

Directions:

1. At 400°F (200°C), preheat your oven.
2. Pierce the sweet potatoes several times with a fork. Place them on a baking sheet.
3. Rub the sweet potatoes with olive oil and sprinkle with black pepper, and salt.
4. Bake them in your preheated oven for about 45-60 minutes.
5. Meanwhile, prepare the chickpea filling. In a suitable-sized skillet, heat a drizzle of olive oil over medium heat.
6. Add the chickpeas, ground cumin, smoked paprika, black pepper, and salt. Sauté for about 5-7 minutes.
7. Remove the sweet potatoes from the oven and let them cool slightly.
8. Slice open the sweet potatoes lengthwise and gently mash the flesh with a fork.
9. In a suitable-sized bowl, mix the hummus and lemon juice to make the hummus dressing.
10. Spoon the chickpea filling onto the sweet potatoes, drizzle hummus dressing, and sprinkle with chopped fresh parsley and green onions.
11. Serve the Stuffed Sweet Potatoes with Hummus Dressing as a flavorful and satisfying meal.

Nutritional Information (per serving): Calories: 461; Fat: 13.2g; Sodium: 145mg; Carbs: 75g; Fibers: 16.2g; Sugar: 5.7g; Proteins: 14.1g

82. Veggie & Hummus Sandwich

Prep time: 10 minutes. | **Cook time:** 0 minutes. | Serves: 2

Ingredients:

- 4 slices of whole-grain bread
- ¼ cup hummus
- 1 small cucumber, thinly sliced
- 1 medium tomato, thinly sliced
- ½ avocado, sliced
- Handful of baby spinach or mixed greens
- Black pepper, and salt, as required

Directions:

1. Lay out the four slices of bread on a clean surface.
2. Spread a generous amount of hummus on two slices of bread.
3. Layer the cucumber slices, tomato slices, avocado slices, and baby spinach or mixed greens on top of the hummus.
4. Sprinkle with black pepper, and salt, as required.
5. Place the remaining two slices of bread on top of the vegetables to form sandwiches.
6. Cut the sandwiches diagonally to create triangles or into halves.
7. Serve the Veggie & Hummus Sandwiches as a wholesome and satisfying lunch or snack option. Enjoy!

Nutritional Information (per serving): Calories: 461; Fat: 13.2g; Sodium: 145mg; Carbs: 75g; Fibers: 16.2g; Sugar: 5.7g; Proteins: 14.1g

83. Roasted Vegetable & Black Bean Tacos

Prep time: 10 minutes. | **Cook time:** 30 minutes. | **Serves:** 4

Ingredients:

- 2 cups mixed vegetables (bell peppers, onions, zucchini), sliced
- 1 tablespoon olive oil
- Black pepper, and salt, as required
- 1 can (15 oz.) black beans, rinsed and drained
- 1 teaspoon (ground) cumin
- ½ teaspoon chili powder
- ¼ teaspoon garlic powder
- ¼ teaspoon paprika
- 8 small tortillas
- Toppings: diced avocado, salsa, chopped cilantro, lime wedges

Directions:

1. At 400°F (200°C), preheat your oven.
2. In a suitable-sized baking sheet, toss the mixed vegetables with olive oil, black pepper, and salt.
3. Spread the vegetables out in a single layer on the baking sheet.
4. Roast for 20-25 minutes in a preheated oven.
5. In a small saucepan, mix the black beans, ground cumin, chili powder, garlic powder, and paprika. Heat over medium heat until the beans are warmed through.
6. Warm the tortillas according to package instructions.
7. Assemble the tacos by spreading a spoonful of black beans on each tortilla, followed by roasted vegetables.
8. Top with diced avocado, salsa, chopped cilantro, and squeeze fresh lime juice over the tacos.
9. Serve the Roasted Vegetable & Black Bean Tacos as a delicious and satisfying meal.

Nutritional Information (per serving): Calories: 240; Fat: 5.6g; Sodium: 301mg; Carbs: 41g; Fibers: 11.7g; Sugar: 0.5g; Proteins: 8.5g

84. Mushroom & Tofu Stir-Fry

Prep time: 30 minutes. | **Cook time:** 10 minutes. | **Serves:** 2

Ingredients:

- 8 oz. firm tofu, cubed
- 2 tablespoons (low-sodium) soy sauce
- 1 tablespoon sesame oil
- 2 tablespoons vegetable oil
- 1 small onion, sliced
- 8 oz. mushrooms, sliced
- 1 red bell pepper, sliced
- 2 cloves garlic, minced
- 1 tablespoon grated ginger
- 2 tablespoons (low-sodium) oyster sauce
- Black pepper, and salt, as required
- Cooked rice or noodles for serving
- Chopped green onions for garnish

Directions:

1. In a bowl, mix the cubed tofu, (low-sodium) soy sauce, and sesame oil. Let 10-15 minutes for the tofu to marinade.
2. Heat vegetable oil in a suitable-sized skillet or wok over medium-high heat.
3. Add the marinated tofu to the skillet and cook until golden brown on all sides. Remove from the skillet and set aside.
4. In the same skillet, add the sliced onion, mushrooms, and red bell pepper. Stir-fry for about 3-4 minutes until the vegetables are tender-crisp.
5. Add the garlic mince and grated ginger to the skillet. Stir-fry for an additional 1 minute.
6. Return the tofu to the skillet and add oyster sauce. Season with black pepper and salt to taste. Stir-fry for another 2 minutes to thoroughly heat everything.
7. Serve the Mushroom & Tofu Stir-Fry over cooked rice or noodles.
8. Garnish with chopped green onions.
9. Enjoy this flavorful and protein-packed stir-fry as a delicious meal.

Nutritional Information (per serving): Calories: 306; Fat: 23.7g; Sodium: 330mg; Carbs: 17.1g; Fibers: 3.8g; Sugar: 7.2g; Proteins: 11.2g

85. Roasted Root Veggies & Greens over Spiced Lentils

Prep time: 10 minutes. | **Cook time:** 30 minutes. | **Serves:** 4

Ingredients:

- 2 cups mixed root vegetables (carrots, parsnips, sweet potatoes), peeled and cubed
- 2 tablespoons olive oil
- Black pepper, and salt, as required
- 1 cup cooked lentils
- ½ teaspoon (ground) cumin
- ½ teaspoon (ground) paprika
- ¼ teaspoon (ground) turmeric
- 4 cups fresh greens (spinach, kale, or Swiss chard)
- 1 tablespoon lemon juice
- Crumbled feta cheese for serving

Directions:

1. At 400°F (200°C), preheat your oven.
2. In a suitable-sized baking sheet, toss the root vegetables with olive oil, black pepper, and salt.
3. Spread the vegetables out in a single layer on the baking sheet.
4. Roast for 20-25 minutes in a preheated oven.
5. In a small saucepan, mix the cooked lentils, ground cumin, ground paprika, and ground turmeric. Heat over medium heat until the lentils are warmed through and the spices are well incorporated.
6. In a separate skillet, heat a drizzle of olive oil over medium heat. Add the fresh greens and cook until wilted.
7. Drizzle the wilted greens with lemon juice and season with black pepper and salt to taste.
8. To serve, spoon the spiced lentils onto a plate or bowl. Top with the roasted root vegetables and wilted greens.
9. Sprinkle with crumbled feta cheese if desired.
10. Enjoy the Roasted Root Veggies & Greens over Spiced Lentils as a nourishing and flavorful meal.

Nutritional Information (per serving): Calories: 293; Fat: 8.1g; Sodium: 26mg; Carbs: 40.9g; Fibers: 19.1g; Sugar: 5.7g; Proteins: 13.3g

86. Quinoa, Avocado & Chickpea Salad over Mixed Greens

Prep time: 10 minutes. | **Cook time:** 0 minutes. | **Serves:** 4

Ingredients:

- 1 cup cooked quinoa
- 1 can (15 oz.) chickpeas, rinsed and drained
- 1 ripe avocado, diced
- 1 cup cherry tomatoes, halved
- ¼ cup chopped red onion
- Juice of 1 lemon
- 2 tablespoons extra-virgin olive oil
- Black pepper, and salt, as required
- 4 cups mixed greens
- Fresh cilantro or parsley for garnish

Directions:

1. In a suitable-sized bowl, mix the cooked quinoa, chickpeas, diced avocado, cherry tomatoes, and chopped red onion.
2. In a suitable-sized bowl, mix the lemon juice, olive oil, black pepper, and salt to make the dressing.
3. Pour the dressing over the quinoa and chickpea mixture. Toss well to combine.
4. Place a bed of mixed greens on each serving plate.
5. Spoon the quinoa, avocado, and chickpea salad over the mixed greens.
6. Garnish with cilantro or parsley.
7. Serve the Quinoa, Avocado & Chickpea Salad over Mixed Greens as a refreshing and nutritious meal.

Nutritional Information (per serving): Calories: 415; Fat: 19.2g; Sodium: 75mg; Carbs: 51.6g; Fibers: 16.5g; Sugar: 9.4g; Proteins: 12.3g

87. Vegan Butternut Squash Carbonara

Prep time: 15 minutes. | **Cook time:** 35 minutes. | **Serves:** 4

Ingredients:

- 8 oz. whole wheat spaghetti or pasta of your choice
- 2 cups cubed butternut squash
- 2 tablespoons olive oil
- ½ cup almond milk
- ¼ cup nutritional yeast
- 1 teaspoon garlic powder
- ½ teaspoon smoked paprika
- Black pepper, and salt, as required
- Chopped fresh parsley for garnish

Directions:

1. Cook the spaghetti as per package instructions until al dente. Drain once cooked then set it aside.
2. At 400°F (200°C), preheat your oven.
3. In a baking sheet, toss the cubed butternut squash with olive oil, black pepper, and salt.
4. Roast the butternut squash in your preheated oven for about 20-25 minutes.
5. In a blender or food processor, mix the roasted butternut squash, plant-based milk, nutritional yeast, garlic powder, smoked paprika, black pepper, and salt. Blend until smooth and creamy.
6. In a suitable-sized skillet, heat up the butternut squash sauce over low heat.
7. Toss the cooked spaghetti in the skillet until it is well coated with the sauce.
8. Cook for a few minutes, stir occasionally, until the pasta is heated through.
9. Serve the Vegan Butternut Squash Carbonara with a sprinkle of chopped fresh parsley on top.
10. Enjoy this creamy and flavorful pasta dish as a satisfying vegan meal.

Nutritional Information (per serving): Calories: 196; Fat: 8.2g; Sodium: 25mg; Carbs: 26.3g; Fibers: 6.3g; Sugar: 2.4g; Proteins: 8.4g

88. Vegan White Bean Chili

Prep time: 10 minutes. | **Cook time:** 40 minutes. | **Serves:** 2

Ingredients:

- 1 tablespoon olive oil
- 1 large onion, chopped
- 3 cloves garlic, minced
- 1 red bell pepper, chopped
- 1 green bell pepper, chopped
- 2 medium carrots, chopped
- 1 can (15 oz.) white beans, rinsed and drained
- 1 can (15 oz.) diced tomatoes
- 2 cups (low-sodium) vegetable broth
- 1 tablespoon chili powder
- 1 teaspoon (ground) cumin
- ½ teaspoon smoked paprika
- Black pepper, and salt, as required
- Fresh cilantro for garnish

Directions:

1. In a suitable-sized pot or Dutch oven, heat up the olive oil over medium heat.
2. To the pot, add the minced onion and garlic. Cook for around 5 minutes.
3. Toss in the chopped red and green bell peppers and carrots to the pot. Cook for another 5 minutes, stir occasionally.
4. Add the white beans, diced tomatoes (with their juices), vegetable broth, chili powder, ground cumin, smoked paprika, black pepper, and salt to the pot. Mix well to combine.
5. Cook the chili to a boil, then reduce its heat to low and simmer for about 20-30 minutes.
6. Taste and adjust the seasonings as needed.
7. Serve the Vegan White Bean Chili hot, garnished with fresh cilantro.
8. Enjoy this hearty and comforting chili as a satisfying vegan meal.

Nutritional Information (per serving): Calories: 354; Fat: 10.4g; Sodium: 394mg; Carbs: 52.5g; Fibers: 17.3g; Sugar: 13g; Proteins: 16.9g

Snacks

89. Homemade Multi-Seed Crackers

Prep time: 10 minutes. | **Cook time:** 20 minutes. | **Serves:** 4

Ingredients:

- 1 cup whole wheat flour
- ¼ cup sesame seeds
- ¼ cup flaxseeds
- ¼ cup sunflower seeds
- ¼ cup pumpkin seeds
- ¼ cup chia seeds
- ½ teaspoon salt
- 2 tablespoons olive oil
- ½ cup water

Directions:

1. At 350°F (175°C), preheat your oven and line a baking sheet with parchment paper.
2. In a mixing bowl, mix the whole wheat flour, sesame seeds, flaxseeds, sunflower seeds, pumpkin seeds, chia seeds, and salt.
3. Add the olive oil and water to the bowl. Mix well until a dough forms.
4. Transfer the dough to a lightly floured surface and roll it out into a thin sheet, about 1/8 inch thick.
5. Using a sharp knife or a pizza cutter, cut the dough into small square or rectangular shapes to form crackers.
6. Transfer the crackers to the prepared baking sheet, leaving a little space between each one.
7. Bake them in your preheated oven for 15-20 minutes.
8. Remove from the oven and let the crackers cool completely on a wire rack.
9. Store the Homemade Multi-Seed Crackers in an airtight container for up to 1 week.
10. Enjoy these nutritious and crunchy crackers as a healthy snack or serve them with your favorite dips or spreads.

Nutritional Information (per serving): Calories: 334; Fat: 20g; Sodium: 297mg; Carbs: 30.8g; Fibers: 5g; Sugar: 0.4g; Proteins: 9.1g

90. Mini Bell Pepper Pebre

Prep time: 10 minutes. | **Cook time:** 30 minutes. | **Serves:** 2

Ingredients:

- 4-5 mini bell peppers, various colors, seeded and diced
- ¼ cup finely chopped red onion
- 2 tablespoons chopped fresh cilantro
- 1 tablespoon chopped fresh parsley
- 1 tablespoon fresh lemon juice
- 2 tablespoons extra-virgin olive oil
- ½ teaspoon (ground) cumin
- Black pepper, and salt, as required

Directions:

1. In a bowl, mix the diced mini bell peppers, red onion, cilantro, parsley, lemon juice, olive oil, ground cumin, black pepper, and salt.
2. Toss the ingredients until well combined.
3. Let the Mini Bell Pepper Pebre sit at room temperature for about 15-20 minutes to allow the flavors to meld.
4. Taste and adjust the seasonings if needed.
5. Serve the Mini Bell Pepper Pebre as a fresh and vibrant salsa or topping for grilled meats, fish, tacos, or salads.
6. Enjoy the burst of flavors and colors in this delicious pebre.

Nutritional Information (per serving): Calories: 178; Fat: 14.6g; Sodium: 11mg; Carbs: 12.9g; Fibers: 4.5g; Sugar: 6.4g; Proteins: 2.4g

91. Pimiento Cheese-Stuffed Mini Bell Peppers

Prep time: 10 minutes. | **Cook time:** 20 minutes. | **Serves:** 5

Ingredients:

- 8-10 mini bell peppers, various colors
- 1 cup shredded low-fat cheddar cheese
- ¼ cup low-fat mayonnaise
- ¼ cup diced pimientos (from a jar)
- ½ teaspoon garlic powder
- Black pepper, and salt, as required
- Chopped fresh chives or parsley for garnish

Directions:

1. At 350°F (175°C), preheat your oven and line a baking sheet with parchment paper.
2. Cut a slit lengthwise in each mini bell pepper, leaving the stem intact. Remove any seeds and pith from the peppers.
3. In a bowl, mix the shredded cheddar cheese, mayonnaise, diced pimientos, garlic powder, black pepper, and salt. Stir well until all of the ingredients are uniformly incorporated.
4. Stuff each mini bell pepper with the pimiento cheese mixture, filling them to the top.
5. Place the stuffed peppers on the prepared baking sheet.
6. Bake them in your preheated oven for 15-20 minutes.
7. Remove from the oven and let the Pimiento Cheese-Stuffed Mini Bell Peppers cool slightly.
8. Garnish with chopped fresh chives or parsley if desired.
9. Serve these delightful and flavorful stuffed peppers as appetizers or as a party snack.
10. Enjoy the combination of the sweet mini bell peppers and creamy pimiento cheese filling.

Nutritional Information (per serving): Calories: 190; Fat: 11.4g; Sodium: 224mg; Carbs: 13.8g; Fibers: 2.1g; Sugar: 7.2g; Proteins: 7.9g

92. Smoked Trout Spread

Prep time: 10 minutes. | **Cook time:** 0 minutes. | **Serves:** 4

Ingredients:

- 8 oz. smoked trout, skin and bones removed
- 4 oz. low-fat cream cheese, softened
- 2 tablespoons low-fat mayonnaise
- 1 tablespoon lemon juice
- 1 tablespoon chopped fresh dill
- 1 tablespoon chopped fresh chives
- Black pepper, and salt, as required
- Crackers or sliced baguette, for serving

Directions:

1. In a bowl, flake the smoked trout into small pieces using a fork.
2. Add the softened cream cheese, mayonnaise, lemon juice, chopped dill, and chopped chives to the bowl.
3. Stir the mixture well until all the ingredients are thoroughly combined.
4. Season with black pepper and salt to taste.
5. Transfer the Smoked Trout Spread to a serving dish.
6. Serve with crackers or sliced baguette.
7. Enjoy this flavorful and creamy spread as an appetizer or snack.

Nutritional Information (per serving): Calories: 239; Fat: 17.2g; Sodium: 177mg; Carbs: 3.1g; Fibers: 0.2g; Sugar: 0.6g; Proteins: 17.5g

93. Roasted Tomatillo Salsa

Prep time: 10 minutes. | **Cook time:** 10 minutes. | **Serves:** 2

Ingredients:

- 1 lb. tomatillos, husked and rinsed
- 1 small onion, quartered
- 2 cloves garlic
- 1 jalapeño pepper, stemmed and seeded
- Juice of 1 lime
- ¼ cup chopped fresh cilantro
- Salt to taste

Directions:

1. Preheat the broiler in your oven.
2. Place the tomatillos, onion quarters, garlic cloves, and jalapeño pepper on a baking sheet.
3. Broil the vegetables for 5-7 minutes, turning them occasionally, until browned and softened.
4. Remove the baking sheet from the oven and let the vegetables cool slightly.
5. In a blender or food processor, mix the roasted tomatillos, onion, garlic, jalapeño pepper, lime juice, chopped cilantro, and a pinch of salt.
6. Blend the ingredients until you achieve your desired salsa consistency. If you prefer a chunkier salsa, pulse the mixture a few times.
7. Taste and adjust the seasoning with more salt if needed.
8. Transfer the Roasted Tomatillo Salsa to a bowl.
9. Let the salsa sit for at least 30 minutes to allow the flavors to meld.
10. Serve the salsa with tortilla chips or as a condiment for tacos, grilled meats, or roasted vegetables.
11. Enjoy the tangy and slightly spicy flavors of this delicious salsa.

Nutritional Information (per serving): Calories: 94; Fat: 2.4g; Sodium: 5mg; Carbs: 18g; Fibers: 5.4g; Sugar: 1.8g; Proteins: 2.9g

94. Radishes with Green Goddess Dressing

Prep time: 10 minutes. | **Cook time:** 15 minutes. | **Serves:** 2

Ingredients:

- 1 bunch radishes, trimmed and sliced
- ½ cup plain Greek yogurt
- 2 tablespoons chopped fresh parsley
- 2 tablespoons chopped fresh chives
- 1 tablespoon chopped fresh tarragon
- 1 tablespoon lemon juice
- 1 clove garlic, minced
- Black pepper, and salt, as required

Directions:

1. In a bowl, mix the sliced radishes.
2. In a separate bowl, mix the Greek yogurt, chopped parsley, chopped chives, chopped tarragon, lemon juice, garlic mince, black pepper, and salt.
3. Pour the green goddess dressing over the sliced radishes.
4. Toss the radishes in the dressing until well covered.
5. Let the radishes with green goddess dressing sit for about 10-15 minutes to allow the flavors to meld.
6. Serve as a light salad or as a pleasant side dish.
7. Enjoy the crisp and peppery radishes paired with the creamy and herby green goddess dressing.

Nutritional Information (per serving): Calories: 86; Fat: 1.2g; Sodium: 120mg; Carbs: 11.6g; Fibers: 4.1g; Sugar: 6.3g; Proteins: 7.9g

95.Baked Parsnip Chips

Prep time: 10 minutes. | **Cook time:** 20 minutes. | **Serves:** 2

Ingredients:

- 2 large parsnips
- 1 tablespoon olive oil
- ½ teaspoon paprika
- ½ teaspoon garlic powder
- Black pepper, and salt, as required

Directions:

1. At 400°F (200°C), preheat your oven and line a baking sheet with parchment paper.
2. Peel the parsnips and slice them into thin rounds using a Mandoline slicer or a sharp knife.
3. In a bowl, toss the parsnip slices with olive oil, paprika, garlic powder, black pepper, and salt until well coated.
4. Arrange the parsnip slices in a single layer on the prepared baking sheet.
5. Bake them in your preheated oven for 15-20 minutes. Halfway through the baking time, flip the chips.
6. Remove from the oven and let the baked parsnip chips cool completely to allow them to crisp up further.
7. Serve as a healthier alternative to potato chips or as a crunchy snack on their own.
8. Enjoy these delicious and guilt-free parsnip chips.

Nutritional Information (per serving): Calories: 164; Fat: 7.5g; Sodium: 14mg; Carbs: 24.7g; Fibers: 6.8g; Sugar: 6.6g; Proteins: 1.8g

96.Baked Zucchini Waffle Fries with Creamy Herb Dip

Prep time: 10 minutes. | **Cook time:** 25 minutes. | **Serves:** 2

Ingredients:

- For the fries:
- 2 medium zucchinis
- ¼ cup bread crumbs
- ¼ cup low-fat parmesan cheese, grated

- ½ teaspoon garlic powder
- ½ teaspoon paprika
- Black pepper, and salt, as required
- Cooking spray
- For the dip:
- ½ cup Greek yogurt
- 1 tablespoon chopped fresh dill
- 1 tablespoon chopped fresh parsley
- 1 tablespoon chopped fresh chives
- 1 clove garlic, minced
- Black pepper, and salt, as required

Directions:

1. At 425°F (220°C), preheat your oven and line a baking sheet with parchment paper.
2. Cut the zucchinis into thick waffle fry-shaped pieces.
3. In a shallow dish, mix the bread crumbs, grated Parmesan cheese, garlic powder, paprika, black pepper, and salt.
4. Dip each zucchini fry into the bread crumb mixture, pressing it down gently to coat all sides.
5. Place the coated zucchini fries on the prepared baking sheet.
6. Lightly spray the fries with cooking spray to help them crisp up.
7. Bake them in your preheated oven for 20-25 minutes. Halfway through the baking time, flip the fries.
8. Meanwhile, prepare the creamy herb dip by combining the Greek yogurt, chopped dill, chopped parsley, chopped chives, garlic mince, black pepper, and salt in a bowl. Mix well.
9. Once the fries are ready, remove them from the oven and let them cool slightly.
10. Serve the baked zucchini waffle fries with the creamy herb dip as a delicious and healthier alternative to traditional fries.
11. Enjoy the crispy fries with the creamy and herby dip.

Nutritional Information (per serving): Calories: 181; Fat: 5.3g; Sodium: 299mg; Carbs: 20.2g; Fibers: 3.4g; Sugar: 6.5g; Proteins: 13.8g

97. Pomegranate Salsa with Pistachios

Prep time: 30 minutes. | **Cook time:** 20 minutes. |
Serves: 8

Ingredients:

- 6 tablespoons sherry vinegar
- 1 medium-sized red onion, sliced
- ¼ cup extra-virgin olive oil
- 1 (½-ounce) fresh serrano chile
- 2 (4-inch) thyme sprigs
- ¼ teaspoon kosher salt
- ¼ teaspoon black pepper
- 1 ½ cups fresh pomegranate arils
- ¼ cup chopped roasted pistachios
- 2 tablespoons chopped fresh chives
- 2 tablespoons chopped fresh flat-leaf parsley

Directions:

1. .Add sherry vinegar to a suitable pan and heat it for 3 minutes until it is reduced to half then keep it aside.
2. Now sauté onion slices with 1 tbsp. olive oil, thyme, black pepper, salt and chile for 6 minutes.
3. Transfer this onion mixture to a cutting board, let it cool then finely chop the onion.
4. Toss pomegranate arils with remaining oil, parsley, pistachios, chives and sherry vinegar reduction in any rightly-sized salad bowl.
5. Stir in the chopped onion mixture, mix well and serve.

Nutritional Information (per serving): Calories: 101; Fat: 8.4g; Sodium: 93mg; Carbs: 7g; Fiber 1.3g; Sugars 3.2g; Protein 1.3g

98. Chili-Lime Brussels Sprout Chips

Prep time: 10 minutes. | **Cook time:** 20 minutes. |
Serves: 4

Ingredients:

- 1 lb. Brussels sprouts
- 2 tablespoons olive oil
- 1 teaspoon chili powder
- ½ teaspoon garlic powder
- ½ teaspoon onion powder
- ½ teaspoon paprika
- ½ teaspoon cumin
- ½ teaspoon salt
- ¼ teaspoon black pepper
- Zest of 1 lime
- Juice of 1 lime

Directions:

1. At 375°F (190°C), preheat your oven and line a baking sheet with parchment paper.
2. Wash the Brussels sprouts and remove any outer leaves that are wilted or damaged. Trim the ends of the sprouts and cut them in half.
3. In a suitable-sized bowl, mix the olive oil, chili powder, garlic powder, onion powder, paprika, cumin, salt, black pepper, lime zest, and lime juice. Mix well to create a marinade.
4. Add the Brussels sprouts to the bowl and toss them in the marinade until they are well coated.
5. Arrange the Brussels sprouts in a single layer on the prepared baking sheet.
6. Place the baking sheet in your preheated oven and bake for about 15-20 minutes.
7. Once the Brussels sprout chips are done, remove them from the oven and let them cool slightly.
8. Serve the chips as a delicious and healthy snack or as a side dish. Enjoy!

Nutritional Information (per serving): Calories: 115; Fat: 7.6g; Sodium: 326mg; Carbs: 11.5g; Fibers: 4.7g; Sugar: 2.7g; Proteins: 4.1g

Desserts

99. Banana Mousse

Prep time: 1 hr. 5 minutes. | **Cook time:** 0 minutes. | **Serves:** 2

Ingredients:

- 2 ripe bananas
- 1 cup low-fat cream
- ¼ cup coconut sugar
- 1 teaspoon vanilla extract
- Optional toppings: sliced bananas, chocolate shavings, or crushed nuts

Directions:

1. Peel and slice the ripe bananas. Blend in a blender or food processor until smooth.
2. In a separate bowl, whip the low-fat cream, coconut sugar, and vanilla extract until stiff peaks form.
3. Gently fold the banana puree into the whipped cream until well combined.
4. Divide the banana mousse into serving glasses or bowls.
5. Refrigerate the mousse for at least 1 hour to allow it to set.
6. Before serving, you can garnish the mousse with sliced bananas, chocolate shavings, or crushed nuts if desired.

Nutritional Information (per serving): Calories: 376; Fat: 22.6g; Sodium: 24mg; Carbs: 43.8g; Fibers: 3.1g; Sugar: 29.5g; Proteins: 2.5g

100. Chocolate Bark with Espresso and Toasted Nuts

Prep time: 10 minutes. | **Cook time:** 5 minutes. | **Serves:** 4

Ingredients:

- 8 oz. dark chocolate, chopped
- 1 tablespoon instant espresso powder
- ½ cup toasted nuts (almonds, walnuts, or hazelnuts), roughly chopped
- Sea salt, for sprinkling

Directions:

1. Line a baking sheet with parchment paper.
2. Melt the dark chocolate in a heatproof bowl set over a pot of simmering water, stirring until smooth.
3. Stir in the instant espresso powder until well incorporated.
4. Spread the melted chocolate evenly over the prepared baking sheet with a spatula.
5. Sprinkle the toasted nuts evenly over the chocolate, pressing them gently into the surface.
6. If desired, sprinkle a small amount of sea salt over the bark for a touch of saltiness.
7. Refrigerate the baking sheet for roughly 1 hour.
8. Once set, break the chocolate bark into pieces of desired size.
9. Store the chocolate bark in an airtight container at room temperature or in the refrigerator.
10. Serve.

Nutritional Information (per serving): Calories: 405; Fat: 25.6g; Sodium: 159mg; Carbs: 38g; Fibers: 3.5g; Sugar: 20g; Proteins: 7.3g

101. Dark Chocolate Frozen Banana Bites

Prep time: 10 minutes. | **Cook time:** 5 minutes. | **Serves:** 4

Ingredients:

- 2 ripe bananas, peeled and cut into bite-sized slices
- 4 oz. dark chocolate, chopped
- Toppings of your choice (crushed nuts, shredded coconut, or sprinkles)

Directions:

1. Line a baking sheet with parchment paper.
2. Place the banana slices on the prepared baking sheet and freeze them for about 30 minutes to 1 hour.
3. Melt the dark chocolate in a heatproof bowl set over a pot of simmering water, stirring until smooth.

4. Using a fork or toothpick, dip each frozen banana slice into the melted chocolate, coating it completely.
5. Allow any excess chocolate to drip off, then place the coated banana slice back onto the baking sheet.
6. Sprinkle the toppings of your choice over the chocolate-coated banana slices.
7. Repeat the same process until all the banana slices are coated.
8. Place the baking sheet in the freezer and freeze the banana bites for at least 2 hours.
9. Once frozen, transfer the banana bites to an airtight container or freezer bag and store them in the freezer until ready to enjoy.
10. Serve the frozen banana bites straight from the freezer as a refreshing and indulgent treat.

Nutritional Information (per serving): Calories: 204; Fat: 8.6g; Sodium: 23mg; Carbs: 30.3g; Fibers: 2.5g; Sugar: 21.8g; Proteins: 2.8g

102. Blueberry Gratin

Prep time: 10 minutes. | **Cook time:** 30 minutes. | **Serves:** 6

Ingredients:

- 4 cups fresh blueberries
- ¼ cup granulated Erythritol
- 1 tablespoon lemon juice
- 1 teaspoon vanilla extract
- 1 cup whole wheat flour
- ½ cup rolled oats
- ½ cup brown Swerve
- ½ teaspoon (ground) cinnamon
- ¼ teaspoon salt
- ½ cup almond butter

Directions:

1. At 375°F (190°C), preheat your oven.
2. Grease a baking dish or individual ramekins with butter or cooking spray.
3. In a suitable-sized bowl, mix the blueberries, granulated sugar, lemon juice, and vanilla extract. Toss gently to coat the blueberries evenly. Transfer the blueberry mixture to the prepared baking dish or divide it among the ramekins.

4. In a separate bowl, mix the flour, rolled oats, brown sugar, cinnamon, and salt. Add the cold butter pieces to the bowl and cut them into the dry ingredients with your fingertips or a pastry cutter. Continue until the mixture resembles coarse crumbs.
5. Sprinkle the crumb mixture evenly over the blueberries in the baking dish or ramekins.
6. Place the dish or ramekins in your preheated oven and bake for about 25-30 minutes.
7. Remove from the oven and set aside to cool. Serve the blueberry gratin warm.

Nutritional Information (per serving): Calories: 170; Fat: 1.7g; Sodium: 99mg; Carbs: 45.7g; Fiber 3.8g; Sugars 19.9g; Protein 4.1g

103. Buckwheat Crepes

Prep time: 10 minutes. | **Cook time:** 10 minutes. | **Serves:** 6

Ingredients:

- 1 cup buckwheat flour
- ½ cup whole-wheat flour
- 2 tablespoons sugar
- ½ teaspoon salt
- 2 cups almond milk
- 2 large eggs
- 2 tablespoons melted almond butter, plus more for greasing the pan

Directions:

1. In a suitable-sized bowl, mix the buckwheat flour, whole-wheat flour, sugar, and salt.
2. In a separate bowl, mix the milk, eggs, and melted butter.
3. Gradually pour the milk mixture into the dry ingredients while mixing continuously until you have a smooth batter. Let the prepared batter rest for about 15-20 minutes.
4. Heat any suitable non-stick skillet or crepe pan over medium heat. Lightly grease the pan with melted butter.
5. Pour about ¼ cup of the prepared batter into the center of the hot pan and swirl it around to evenly coat the bottom.

6. Cook the crepe for about 2 minutes. Flip the crepe using a spatula and cook for an additional 1-2 minutes on the other side.
7. To keep the crepe warm, place it on a dish and cover it with a clean kitchen towel.
8. Repeat the same process with the remaining batter, greasing the pan lightly between each crepe.
9. Serve the buckwheat crepes warm with your favorite fillings and toppings, fresh fruit, whipped cream, Nutella, or maple syrup.

Nutritional Information (per serving): Calories: 218; Fat: 7.9g; Sodium: 285mg; Carbs: 30.2g; Fibers: 2.3g; Sugar: 8.4g; Proteins: 8.4g

104. Caramelized Pineapple with Raspberries

Prep time: 10 minutes.| **Cook time:** 10 minutes.| **Serves:** 2

Ingredients:

- 1 ripe pineapple, peeled, cored, and cut into slices or chunks
- ¼ cup brown sugar
- 2 tablespoons almond butter
- 1 cup fresh raspberries

Directions:

1. Heat a suitable-sized skillet or frying pan over medium heat.
2. Add the butter to the pan and let it melt. Sprinkle the brown sugar evenly over the melted butter.
3. Place the pineapple slices or chunks in the pan and cook for about 3-4 minutes per side.
4. Remove the caramelized pineapple from the pan and transfer it to a serving plate.
5. Sprinkle the fresh raspberries over the caramelized pineapple.
6. Serve the caramelized pineapple with raspberries as a sweet and tangy dessert. You can enjoy it on its own or pair it with a scoop of vanilla ice cream or a dollop of whipped cream if desired.

Nutritional Information (per serving): Calories: 285; Fat: 12.1g; Sodium: 90mg; Carbs: 46.8g; Fibers: 6.3g; Sugar: 36.6g; Proteins: 1.8g

105. Raspberry Banana Sorbet

Prep time: 10 minutes.| **Cook time:** 0 minutes.| **Serves:** 4

Ingredients:

- 2 ripe bananas, peeled and frozen
- 2 cups frozen raspberries
- 1-2 tablespoons honey (for added sweetness)

Directions:

1. Place the frozen bananas and frozen raspberries in a blender or food processor.
2. Blend the fruits until smooth and creamy. You may need to stop and scrape down the sides of the blender or processor to ensure even blending.
3. If desired, add honey to the mixture for added sweetness. Blend again until well combined.
4. Once the sorbet reaches a smooth and creamy consistency, transfer it to a container and freeze for about 1-2 hours to firm up.
5. Serve the raspberry banana sorbet in bowls or cones for a refreshing and fruity dessert.

Nutritional Information (per serving): Calories: 197; Fat: 0.4g; Sodium: 2mg; Carbs: 50.5g; Fibers: 7g; Sugar: 38.7g; Proteins: 1.5g

106. Chia Pudding

Prep time: 2 hrs. 10 minutes.| **Cook time:** 0 minutes.| **Serves:** 4

Ingredients:

- ¼ cup chia seeds
- 1 cup almond milk
- 1-2 tablespoons honey (for sweetness)
- ½ teaspoon vanilla extract
- Toppings of your choice (fresh fruit, nuts, or granola)

Directions:

1. In a bowl, mix the chia seeds, milk, honey, and vanilla extract. Mix well to evenly distribute the chia seeds.
2. Let the mixture to sit for 5 minutes before stirring again to prevent clumping.
3. Cover the bowl and refrigerate the chia pudding for at least 2 hours or overnight, allowing the chia

seeds to absorb the liquid and create a pudding-like texture.

4. After the pudding has set, give it a stir to break up any clumps that may have formed.
5. Spoon the chia pudding into serving bowls or jars and top with your favorite toppings, fresh fruit, nuts, or granola.
6. Enjoy the chia pudding as a nutritious and customizable breakfast, snack, or dessert.

Nutritional Information (per serving): Calories: 117; Fat: 5.6g; Sodium: 31mg; Carbs: 13.4g; Fibers: 4.9g; Sugar: 7.1g; Proteins: 4.4g

107. Dark Chocolate and Cherry Brownies

Prep time: 10 minutes. | **Cook time:** 30 minutes. | **Serves:** 8

Ingredients:

- 1 cup dark chocolate, chopped
- ½ cup almond butter
- 3/4 cup coconut sugar
- 2 large eggs
- 1 teaspoon vanilla extract
- ½ cup whole-wheat flour
- ¼ cup unsweetened cocoa powder
- ¼ teaspoon salt
- 1 cup fresh or frozen cherries, pitted and halved

Directions:

1. At 350°F (175°C), preheat your oven. Grease or line a square baking pan with parchment paper.
2. In a heatproof bowl, melt the dark chocolate and butter together, either over a pot of simmering water or in the microwave, stirring until smooth. Set aside to cool slightly.
3. In a separate large bowl, mix the sugar, eggs, and vanilla extract until well combined.
4. Pour the melted chocolate mixture into the egg mixture and mix until smooth.
5. In a separate bowl, mix the flour, cocoa powder, and salt.
6. Gradually stir in the dry flour mixture, stirring until just combined.
7. Gently fold in the cherry halves, reserving a few for topping.
8. Pour the prepared batter into the prepared baking pan and spread it out evenly. Top with the

reserved cherry halves, pressing them gently into the prepared batter.
9. Bake it in your preheated oven for about 25-30 minutes.
10. Remove the brownies from the oven and let them cool in the pan before cutting into squares.

Nutritional Information (per serving): Calories: 347; Fat: 19.2g; Sodium: 114mg; Carbs: 42g; Fibers: 2.1g; Sugar: 32.6g; Proteins: 5.7g

108. Avocado Brownies

Prep time: 10 minutes. | **Cook time:** 25 minutes. | **Serves:** 6

Ingredients:

- 2 ripe avocados
- ½ cup unsweetened cocoa powder
- ½ cup honey
- 2 large eggs
- 1 teaspoon vanilla extract
- ½ cup whole wheat flour
- ½ teaspoon baking powder
- ¼ teaspoon salt
- ½ cup dark chocolate chips

Directions:

1. At 350°F (175°C), preheat your oven. Grease or line a baking pan with parchment paper.
2. In a mixing bowl, mash the ripe avocados until smooth and creamy.
3. Add the cocoa powder, honey, eggs, and vanilla extract to the mashed avocados. Mix well to combine.
4. In a separate bowl, mix the flour, baking powder, and salt.
5. Gradually add the dry ingredients to the avocado mixture, stirring until just combined. Be careful not to overmix.
6. If desired, fold in the dark chocolate chips.
7. Pour the prepared batter into the prepared baking pan and spread it out evenly.
8. Bake it in your preheated oven for about 20-25 minutes.
9. Remove the brownies from the oven and let them cool in the pan before cutting into squares. Enjoy

Nutritional Information (per serving): Calories: 350; Fat: 18.5g; Sodium: 128mg; Carbs: 48g; Fibers: 7.2g; Sugar: 29.3g; Proteins: 6.6g

Quick and Easy Meals

109. Honey Glazed Salmon

Prep time: 10 minutes. | **Cook time:** 10 minutes. |
Serves: 4

Ingredients:

- 4 wild caught salmon fillets-½ lb. each
- Black pepper, and salt, to season
- ½ teaspoon paprika
- 2 tablespoons olive oil
- 4 cloves garlic, finely chopped
- 4 tablespoons honey
- 1 tablespoon water
- 2 teaspoons low- sodium soy sauce
- 1 tablespoon fresh squeezed lemon juice
- Lemon wedges to serve

Directions:

1. Position the oven shelf in the middle of your oven. Preheat the oven to medium heat using the broil/grill setting.
2. Season the salmon with salt, pepper, and paprika, and set it aside.
3. In a suitable-sized skillet or pan, heat up the oil over medium-high heat. Sauté the garlic until fragrant, approximately one minute. Then, add the honey, water, and soy sauce, allowing the flavors to combine and heat through. Stir in the lemon juice to blend all the flavors together.
4. Place the salmon steaks in the pan with the sauce, cooking each fillet for 3-4 minutes (skin-side down if applicable), basting the tops with the pan juices. Season with salt and pepper according to your taste.
5. Optionally, add lemon wedges around the salmon for a stronger lemon flavor.
6. Baste the salmon once more, then transfer the pan to the oven to broil/grill for an additional 5-6 minutes, until the tops of the salmon are nicely charred and the salmon is cooked to your desired level.
7. Serve it with the sauce and some lemon juice.

Nutritional Information (per serving): Calories: 243; Fat: 9.1g; Sodium: 526mg; Carbs: 18.4g; Fibers: 0.6g; Sugar: 18.5g; Proteins: 23.3g

110. Bean Burger

Prep time: 5 minutes. | **Cook time:** 25 minutes. |
Serves: 4

Ingredients:

- 1 (15 oz.) can of black beans, drained and rinsed
- 1/3 cup 1 tablespoon gluten-free rolled oats
- 1 large shallot, chopped
- 2 cloves garlic, chopped
- ½ tablespoon old bay seasoning
- Black pepper, to taste

Directions:

1. In the food processor, combine all the ingredients and pulse for 15 to 20 seconds until the mixture starts to come together.
2. Use wet hands to shape the mixture into patties, make four equal sized patties.
3. Place the patties onto the prepared baking sheet and place it in the oven for 15 minutes.
4. Flip the patties over and continue baking for an additional 10 minutes.
5. Serve these patties with your favorite side salad.

Nutritional Information (per serving): Calories: 402; Fat: 2.1g; Sodium: 247mg; Carbs: 73.8g; Fibers: 1.4g; Sugar: 2.3g; Proteins: 24.5g

111. Strawberry Spinach Salad with Avocado & Walnuts

Prep time: 10 minutes. | **Cook time:** 0 minutes. | **Serves:** 6

Ingredients:

- 6 cups fresh spinach leaves
- 1 cup sliced strawberries
- 1 ripe avocado, diced
- ½ cup chopped walnuts
- ¼ cup crumbled feta cheese
- 2 tablespoons balsamic vinegar
- 2 tablespoons extra-virgin olive oil
- 1 tablespoon honey
- Black pepper, and salt, as required

Directions:

1. In a suitable-sized salad bowl, combine spinach, sliced strawberries, diced avocado, chopped walnuts, and crumbled feta cheese.
2. In a suitable-sized bowl, mix balsamic vinegar, olive oil, honey, black pepper, and salt until well combined.
3. Pour the dressing over the salad and gently toss to coat all of the ingredients.
4. Serve immediately as a light and refreshing salad.

Nutritional Information (per serving): Calories: 216; Fat: 18.9g; Sodium: 96mg; Carbs: 10g; Fibers: 4.1g; Sugar: 4.7g; Proteins: 5.1g

112. Grilled Shrimp

Prep time: 5 minutes. | **Cook time:** 10 minutes. | **Serves:** 2

Ingredients:

- 1 lb. large shrimp, peeled and deveined
- 2 tablespoons olive oil
- 1 teaspoon smoked paprika
- ½ teaspoon garlic powder
- Black pepper, and salt, as required

Directions:

8. Preheat the grill or a grill pan over medium-high heat.
9. In a bowl, toss the shrimp with olive oil, smoked paprika, garlic powder, black pepper, and salt until coated.
10. Grill the shrimp for 2-3 minutes per side until they are pink and cooked through. Set aside.
11. Serve the grilled shrimp warm.

Nutritional Information (per serving): Calories: 308; Fat: 14.2g; Sodium: 284mg; Carbs: 5.2g; Fibers: 0.5g; Sugar: 0.3g; Proteins: 42.8g

113. Pan-Seared Steak with Crispy Herbs & Escarole

Prep time: 10 minutes. | **Cook time:** 15 minutes. | **Serves:** 2

Ingredients:

- 2 ribeye or sirloin steaks
- Black pepper, and salt, as required
- 2 tablespoons olive oil
- 4 tablespoons almond butter
- 4 sprigs fresh thyme
- 4 sprigs fresh rosemary
- 2 cloves garlic, minced
- 4 cups escarole leaves, washed and torn
- 1 tablespoon lemon juice

Directions:

1. Season the steaks generously with black pepper, and salt on both sides.
2. Heat olive oil in a suitable-sized skillet over high heat until shimmering.
3. Add the steaks to the hot skillet and sear for about 3-4 minutes per side for medium-rare, or adjust the cooking time to your desired doneness.
4. Reduce its heat to medium and add butter, fresh thyme, fresh rosemary, and garlic mince to the skillet. Let the butter melt and foam.
5. Continuously spoon the herb-infused butter over the steaks for an additional 1-2 minutes to enhance the flavors.
6. Remove the steaks from the skillet and let them rest on a cutting board for a few minutes.
7. In the same skillet, add the torn escarole leaves and cook for about 2-3 minutes until wilted.
8. Squeeze lemon juice over the escarole and season with black pepper and salt to taste.
9. Thinly slice the rested steaks against the grain.

10. Arrange the steak slices on a serving platter alongside the crispy herbs and escarole.
11. Drizzle any remaining herb butter from the skillet over the steak slices.
12. Serve the pan-seared steak with crispy herbs and escarole as a delicious and satisfying main dish.

Nutritional Information (per serving): Calories: 397; Fat: 30.6g; Sodium: 80mg; Carbs: 3.5g; Fibers: 3.1g; Sugar: 0.4g; Proteins: 27.1g

114. Arugula Salad

Prep time: 5 minutes. | **Cook time:** 0 minutes. | **Serves:** 4

Ingredients:

- ¾ cup Parmesan cheese shavings
- 1 small shallot, chopped
- 8 cups (5 oz.) baby arugula
- 2 tablespoons extra virgin olive oil
- ¼ teaspoon kosher salt
- 1 ½ tablespoons lemon juice
- Zest of ½ lemon

Directions:

1. Put the baby arugula, olive oil, optional lemon zest, lemon juice, and kosher salt in a spacious bowl.
2. Stir them together with your hands until they are equally coated.
3. Include the Parmesan shavings and shallot, and give it a quick toss until they are combined.
4. Serve as a refreshing salad

Nutritional Information (per serving): Calories: 99; Fat: 8.8g; Sodium: 241mg; Carbs: 3.3g; Fibers: 0.7g; Sugar: 0.6g; Proteins: 3g

115. Easy Pea & Spinach Carbonara

Prep time: 15 minutes. | **Cook time:** 20 minutes. | **Serves:** 4

Ingredients:

- 8 oz. spaghetti or your choice of pasta
- 2 tablespoons olive oil
- 2 cloves garlic, minced

- 1 cup frozen peas
- 2 cups fresh spinach leaves
- ½ cup low-fat parmesan cheese, grated
- 2 large eggs
- Black pepper, and salt, as required

Directions:

1. Cook the spaghetti or pasta as per package instructions until al dente. Drain once cooked then set it aside.
2. In a suitable-sized skillet, heat olive oil over medium heat.
3. In the same skillet, add garlic mince and cook for 1 minute until fragrant.
4. Stir in frozen peas and cook for another 2 minutes until heated through.
5. Add fresh spinach leaves to the skillet and simmer until wilted.
6. In a suitable-sized bowl, mix grated Parmesan cheese and eggs.
7. Return the cooked spaghetti to the skillet with the pea and spinach mixture. Pour the Parmesan-egg mixture over the pasta and toss well to coat the pasta evenly.
8. Cook for an additional 1-2 minutes until the sauce thickens slightly and coats the pasta.
9. Season with black pepper and salt to taste.
10. Serve the easy pea and spinach carbonara hot.

Nutritional Information (per serving): Calories: 444; Fat: 21.9g; Sodium: 660mg; Carbs: 38.7g; Fibers: 2.6g; Sugar: 2.1g; Proteins: 23.7g

116. Cajun Salmon

Prep time: 5 minutes. | **Cook time:** 10 minutes. | **Serves:** 4

Ingredients:

- 4 salmon fillets
- 2 tablespoons Cajun seasoning
- 2 tablespoons olive oil

Directions:

1. In a suitable-sized bowl, mix all the Cajun seasoning ingredients.
2. Rub the Cajun seasoning evenly on both sides of the salmon fillets.

3. Heat olive oil in a suitable-sized skillet over medium-high heat.
4. Add the salmon fillets to the skillet and cook for about 4-5 minutes per side.
5. Once the salmon is cooked, remove it from the skillet and let it rest for a few minutes.
6. Serve the Cajun salmon hot. Enjoy!

Nutritional Information (per serving): Calories: 296; Fat: 18g; Sodium: 153mg; Carbs: 0g; Fibers: 0g; Sugar: 0g; Proteins: 34.6g

117. Sauteed Asparagus

Prep time: 5 minutes. | **Cook time:** 12 minutes. | Serves: 4

Ingredients:

- ½ tablespoon olive oil
- 1 bunch asparagus, woody ends trimmed
- ½ teaspoon seasoning salt
- ½ teaspoon black pepper

Directions:

1. In a suitable-sized skillet over medium heat, heat olive oil.
2. Place the asparagus in the skillet and generously season with salt and pepper.
3. Sauté the asparagus, tossing occasionally, for a duration of 5-12 minutes. If you desire a crisp and crunchy texture, cook for 5 minutes. For a softer and more tender consistency, cook for approximately 10-12 minutes.

Nutritional Information (per serving): Calories: 43; Fat: 1.8g; Sodium: 293mg; Carbs: 5.4g; Fibers: 2.5g; Sugar: 2.6g; Proteins: 0.8g

118. Grilled Blackened Shrimp

Prep time: 5 minutes. | **Cook time:** 10 minutes. | Serves: 4

Ingredients:

- 1 lb. large shrimp, peeled and deveined
- 2 tablespoons blackened seasoning
- 2 tablespoons olive oil
- **For the blackened seasoning:**

- 1 tablespoon paprika
- 1 teaspoon garlic powder
- 1 teaspoon onion powder
- 1 teaspoon dried thyme
- 1 teaspoon dried oregano
- 1 teaspoon cayenne pepper
- 1 teaspoon smoked paprika
- ¼ teaspoon salt
- ½ teaspoon black pepper

Directions:

1. In a suitable-sized bowl, mix all the blackened seasoning ingredients.
2. Pat the shrimp dry with paper towels and place them in a bowl.
3. Sprinkle the blackened seasoning over the shrimp and toss to coat them evenly.
4. Heat olive oil in a grill pan or skillet over medium-high heat.
5. Add the seasoned shrimp to the pan and cook for 2-3 minutes per side.
6. Serve the grilled blackened shrimp immediately. Enjoy!

Nutritional Information (per serving): Calories: 329; Fat: 14.8g; Sodium: 577mg; Carbs: 9.6g; Fibers: 2.4g; Sugar: 1.3g; Proteins: 43.7g

119. Grilled Salmon with Cilantro-Ginger Sauce

Prep time: 15 minutes. | **Cook time:** 10 minutes. | Serves: 4

Ingredients:

- 4 salmon fillets
- 2 tablespoons olive oil
- Black pepper, and salt, as required
- For the cilantro-ginger sauce:
- 1 cup fresh cilantro leaves
- 2 tablespoons grated ginger
- 2 cloves garlic
- 2 tablespoons lime juice
- 2 tablespoons (low-sodium) soy sauce
- 2 tablespoons honey
- 1 tablespoon sesame oil

Directions:

1. Preheat the grill to medium-high heat.
2. Brush the salmon fillets with olive oil and season with black pepper, and salt.
3. Place the salmon fillets on the grill and cook for about 4-5 minutes per side.
4. While the salmon is grilling, prepare the cilantro-ginger sauce. In a blender or food processor, combine cilantro leaves, grated ginger, garlic, lime juice, soy sauce, honey, and sesame oil. Blend until smooth.
5. Once the salmon is cooked, remove it from the grill and let it rest for a few minutes.
6. Serve the grilled salmon with a drizzle of cilantro-ginger sauce on top. Enjoy!

Nutritional Information (per serving): Calories: 344; Fat: 18.2g; Sodium: 533mg; Carbs: 11.8g; Fibers: 0.6g; Sugar: 8.9g; Proteins: 35.5g

120. One-Pot Garlicky Shrimp & Spinach

Prep time: 10 minutes. | **Cook time:** 10 minutes. | **Serves:** 2

Ingredients:

- 1 lb. shrimp, peeled and deveined
- 2 tablespoons olive oil
- 4 cloves garlic, minced
- 1 teaspoon red pepper flakes
- 4 cups fresh spinach leaves
- 1 cup cherry tomatoes, halved
- 1 tablespoon lemon juice
- Black pepper, and salt, as required

Directions:

1. Heat olive oil in a suitable-sized skillet over medium heat.
2. Add the minced garlic and red pepper flakes to the skillet and heat for 1 minute, or until fragrant.
3. Add shrimp to the skillet and cook for 2-3 minutes per side. Remove the shrimp from the skillet and set aside.
4. In the same skillet, add spinach leaves and cherry tomatoes. Cook for 2-3 minutes until the spinach wilts and the tomatoes soften.
5. Return the cooked shrimp to the skillet and drizzle lemon juice over the ingredients. Season with black pepper and salt to taste.

6. Mix everything until fully combined and thoroughly cooked.
7. Serve the garlicky shrimp and spinach in a bowl. Enjoy!

Nutritional Information (per serving): Calories: 433; Fat: 18.5g; Sodium: 608mg; Carbs: 11.8g; Fibers: 2.8g; Sugar: 2.9g; Proteins: 54.7g

121. Farfalle with Mushrooms and Spinach

Prep time: 10 minutes. | **Cook time:** 15 minutes. | **Serves:** 2

Ingredients:

- 8 oz. farfalle pasta (bowtie pasta)
- 2 tablespoons olive oil
- 8 oz. mushrooms, sliced
- 4 cloves garlic, minced
- 4 cups fresh spinach leaves
- ¼ cup low-fat parmesan cheese, grated
- Black pepper, and salt, as required

Directions:

1. Cook the farfalle pasta as per package instructions until al dente. Drain once cooked then set it aside.
2. In a suitable-sized skillet, heat olive oil over medium heat.
3. Add sliced mushrooms to the skillet and cook for 5-6 minutes until they release their moisture and start to brown.
4. Add garlic mince to the skillet and cook for an additional 1 minute until fragrant.
5. Add fresh spinach leaves to the skillet and cook until wilted.
6. Add the cooked farfalle pasta to the skillet and toss everything to combine.
7. Sprinkle grated Parmesan cheese over the pasta and vegetables. Season with black pepper and salt to taste.
8. Continue to cook for a few minutes until the cheese melts and everything is heated through.
9. Serve the farfalle with mushrooms and spinach as a delicious and comforting pasta dish. Enjoy!

Nutritional Information (per serving): Calories: 362; Fat: 21.1g; Sodium: 315mg; Carbs: 29.4g; Fibers: 3.6g; Sugar: 3.3g; Proteins: 18.2g

Meals on a Budget

122. Thai Chicken Risotto

Prep time: 10 minutes. | **Cook time:** 30 minutes. | **Serves:** 4

Ingredients:

- 1 tablespoon vegetable oil
- 1 onion, finely chopped
- 2 cloves garlic, minced
- 1 red bell pepper, diced
- 1 cup white rice
- 4 cups (low-sodium) chicken broth
- 1 cup coconut milk
- 1 tablespoon Thai red curry paste
- 1 cup cooked chicken, shredded
- 1 cup frozen peas
- 2 tablespoons fish sauce
- Fresh cilantro, chopped (for garnish)
- Black pepper, and salt, as required

Directions:

1. Heat up the vegetable oil in a suitable-sized pot or Dutch oven over medium heat.
2. Toss in the chopped onion, garlic mince, and diced red bell pepper to the pot. Sauté until the vegetables are softened and fragrant.
3. Add the rice to the pot and cook, stirring frequently, for about 2 minutes until the rice is well-coated with the oil and slightly toasted.
4. In a separate saucepan, heat up the chicken broth and coconut milk until hot but not boiling.
5. Add the Thai red curry paste to the pot with the rice and vegetables. Mix well to combine.
6. Gradually add the hot (low-sodium) chicken broth mixture to the pot, about ½ cup at a time, stirring constantly until the liquid is absorbed before adding more.
7. Continue this process of adding the broth mixture and stirring until the rice is creamy and al dente, about 20-25 minutes.
8. Stir in the cooked shredded chicken and frozen peas, and cook for an additional 3-4 minutes until the chicken and peas are heated through.
9. Stir in the lime juice. Season with black pepper and salt to taste.
10. Remove the pot from the heat. Let the risotto rest for a few minutes.
11. Serve the Thai chicken risotto hot, garnished with fresh cilantro. Enjoy!

Nutritional Information (per serving): Calories: 399; Fat: 10.4g; Sodium: 324mg; Carbs: 56g; Fibers: 4.5g; Sugar: 5.6g; Proteins: 22.1g

123. Mozzarella, and Baked Bean Jaffles

Prep time: 10 minutes. | **Cook time:** 10 minutes. | **Serves:** 4

Ingredients:

- 8 slices bread
- 1 cup low-fat mozzarella cheese, shredded
- 1 cup baked beans
- Peanut butter (for spreading)

Directions:

1. Preheat a jaffle maker or sandwich press.
2. Take a slice of bread and spread butter on one side.
3. Place the bread slice, buttered side down, into the jaffle maker.
4. Layer the mozzarella cheese, and baked beans on top of the bread.
5. Place another slice of bread on top, buttered side up.
6. Close your jaffle maker and cook for a few minutes until the bread is toasted and the cheese has melted.
7. Repeat the same process for the remaining bread slices and ingredients.
8. Carefully remove the jaffles from the maker and let them cool slightly before serving.
9. Serve the mozzarella, and baked bean jaffles as a delicious and satisfying snack or meal.

Nutritional Information (per serving): Calories: 266; Fat: 13g; Sodium: 871mg; Carbs: 23.2g; Fibers: 3.9g; Sugar: 0.8g; Proteins: 13.9g

124. Leek and Yoghurt Soup with Slow-Braised Onions

Prep time: 10 minutes. | **Cook time:** 1 hr. 10 minutes. | Serves: 4

Ingredients:

- 2 large leeks, white and light green parts only, thinly sliced
- 2 tablespoons peanut butter
- 1 tablespoon olive oil
- 2 onions, thinly sliced
- 2 cloves garlic, minced
- 4 cups (low-sodium) vegetable broth
- 1 cup plain Greek yogurt
- Black pepper, and salt, as required
- Fresh chives or parsley, chopped (for garnish)

Directions:

1. In a suitable-sized pot, melt the butter and olive oil over medium heat.
2. Add the sliced leeks, onions, and garlic mince to the pot. Cook, stir occasionally, for about 10 minutes until the vegetables are softened and lightly browned.
3. Reduce its heat to low and continue cooking the onions and leeks for an additional 30-40 minutes, stir occasionally.
4. Add the vegetable broth to the pot and increase the heat to medium-high. Cook the soup to a boil, then reduce its heat and simmer for about 10 minutes to allow the flavors to meld.
5. Use an immersion blender or transfer the soup to a blender to puree until smooth.
6. Return the pureed soup to the pot and stir in the Greek yogurt. Heat up the soup gently over low heat, stirring continuously until well combined and warmed through. Do not let it boil.
7. Season the soup with black pepper, and salt, as required.
8. Divide the leek and yoghurt soup into bowls and garnish with chives or parsley.
9. Serve the soup hot and enjoy its creamy, comforting flavors.

Nutritional Information (per serving): Calories: 211; Fat: 11.6g; Sodium: 440mg; Carbs: 15.1g; Fibers: 2g; Sugar: 6.5g; Proteins: 12g

125. Spaghetti in Cherry Tomato Sauce

Prep time: 10 minutes. | **Cook time:** 25 minutes. | Serves: 2

Ingredients:

- 8 oz. spaghetti
- 2 tablespoons olive oil
- 3 cloves garlic, minced
- 1 pint cherry tomatoes, halved
- ¼ cup fresh basil leaves, chopped
- Black pepper, and salt, as required

Directions:

1. Cook the spaghetti as per package instructions until al dente. Drain once cooked then set it aside.
2. In a suitable-sized skillet, heat up the olive oil over medium heat.
3. Add the garlic mince to the skillet and cook for about 1 minute until fragrant.
4. Cook the cherry tomatoes in the pan for 4-5 minutes, or until they begin to soften and release their juices.
5. Use the back of a spoon or a fork to lightly crush some of the tomatoes to release their flavors.
6. Stir in the chopped basil leaves and season with black pepper and salt to taste.
7. Add the cooked spaghetti to the skillet and toss everything until the pasta is well-coated with the cherry tomato sauce.
8. Cook for an additional 2-3 minutes to heat up the pasta through.
9. Serve the spaghetti in cherry tomato sauce hot.

Nutritional Information (per serving): Calories: 470; Fat: 10g; Sodium: 39mg; Carbs: 70.7g; Fibers: 2.3g; Sugar: 4.8g; Proteins: 14.8g

126. Roasted Sweet Potatoes with Chili and Seeds

Prep time: 10 minutes. | **Cook time:** 30 minutes. | **Serves:** 2

Ingredients:

- 2 large sweet potatoes, peeled and cubed
- 2 tablespoons olive oil
- 1 teaspoon chili powder
- ½ teaspoon paprika
- ½ teaspoon cumin
- ½ teaspoon salt
- ¼ teaspoon black pepper
- 2 tablespoons mixed seeds (sesame, pumpkin, or sunflower seeds)

Directions:

1. At 400°F (200°C), preheat your oven.
2. Place the sweet potato cubes in a suitable-sized mixing bowl.
3. In a suitable-sized bowl, mix the olive oil, chili powder, paprika, cumin, salt, and black pepper. Mix well to make a spice mixture.
4. Pour the spice mixture over the sweet potato cubes and toss to coat them evenly.
5. Transfer the seasoned sweet potatoes to a baking sheet and spread them out in a single layer.
6. Roast the sweet potatoes in your preheated oven for 25-30 minutes, flip them halfway through.
7. While the sweet potatoes are roasting, toast the mixed seeds in a dry skillet over medium heat for a few minutes until they become fragrant and lightly browned. Set aside.
8. Once the sweet potatoes are done, remove them from the oven and transfer them to a serving dish.
9. Sprinkle the toasted seeds over the roasted sweet potatoes.
10. Serve the roasted sweet potatoes with chili and seeds as a tasty side dish or a light meal.

Nutritional Information (per serving): Calories: 305; Fat: 14.7g; Sodium: 609mg; Carbs: 43.2g; Fibers: 6.9g; Sugar: 0.9g; Proteins: 2.7g

127. Prawn and Spinach Angel Hair Pasta with Prawn Oil

Prep time: 10 minutes. | **Cook time:** 20 minutes. | **Serves:** 4

Ingredients:

- 8 oz. angel hair pasta
- 1 lb. large prawns, peeled and deveined (shells reserved)
- 3 tablespoons olive oil, divided
- 4 cloves garlic, minced
- ½ teaspoon red pepper flakes
- 4 cups fresh spinach leaves
- ¼ cup chopped fresh parsley
- Black pepper, and salt, as required
- For the prawn oil:
- Reserved prawn shells
- ¼ cup olive oil

Directions:

1. Cook the angel hair pasta as per package instructions until al dente. Drain once cooked then set it aside.
2. In a suitable-sized skillet, heat 1 tablespoon of olive oil over medium heat.
3. Add the prawns to the skillet and cook for 2-3 minutes per side until they turn pink and opaque. Remove the prawns from the skillet and set aside.
4. In the same skillet, heat up the remaining 2 tablespoons of olive oil over medium heat.
5. Add the garlic mince and red pepper flakes to the skillet and cook for 1 minute until fragrant.
6. Add the spinach leaves to the skillet and cook until wilted.
7. Return the cooked prawns to the skillet and add the cooked angel hair pasta. Toss everything until well combined.
8. Stir in the chopped parsley and season with black pepper and salt to taste.
9. For the prawn oil, heat ¼ cup of olive oil in a separate small skillet over medium heat. Add the reserved prawn shells and cook, stir occasionally, for about 5 minutes until the shells turn pink and fragrant. Remove the shells and discard.
10. Drizzle the prawn oil over the prawn and spinach angel hair pasta, and toss to coat.

11. Serve the dish hot, and enjoy the flavors of prawns, spinach, and aromatic prawn oil.

Nutritional Information (per serving): Calories: 344; Fat: 12.8g; Sodium: 42mg; Carbs: 34.4g; Fibers: 1.5g; Sugar: 0.2g; Proteins: 23.8g

128. Beef Spaghetti

Prep time: 15 minutes. | **Cook time:** 30 minutes. | **Serves:** 4

Ingredients:

- 8 oz. spaghetti
- 1 tablespoon olive oil
- 1 lb. (ground) lean beef
- 1 onion, diced
- 2 cloves garlic, minced
- ½ cup ale
- 1 cup tomato sauce
- 1 teaspoon dried oregano
- Black pepper, and salt, as required
- Low-fat parmesan cheese, grated (for serving)
- Fresh parsley, chopped (for garnish)

Directions:

1. Cook the spaghetti as per package instructions until al dente. Drain once cooked then set it aside.
2. In a suitable-sized skillet, add the olive oil and ground lean beef and cook until browned, breaking it up into crumbles. Drain any excess grease.
3. Toss in the diced onion and garlic mince to the skillet with the ground lean beef. Cook the onion for 5 minutes, or until it is transparent.
4. Pour in the ale and allow it to simmer for a few minutes to cook out some of the alcohol.
5. Stir in the tomato sauce and dried oregano. Season with black pepper, and salt, as required.
6. Reduce its heat to low and let the sauce simmer for about 10 minutes to allow the flavors to meld.
7. Add the cooked spaghetti to the skillet and toss everything until the pasta is well coated with the sauce.
8. Serve the beef spaghetti hot, topped with grated Parmesan cheese, and chopped fresh parsley.

Nutritional Information (per serving): Calories: 348; Fat: 10.8g; Sodium: 791mg; Carbs: 39g; Fibers: 1.7g; Sugar: 3.8g; Proteins: 21.3g

129. Broccoli and Cheese Soup with Garlic Cheese Toasts

Prep time: 10 minutes. | **Cook time:** 25 minutes. | **Serves:** 4

Ingredients:

- 2 tablespoons almond butter
- 1 onion, chopped
- 2 cloves garlic, minced
- 4 cups broccoli florets
- 4 cups (low-sodium) vegetable broth
- 1 cup grated low-fat cheddar cheese
- ½ cup low-fat cream
- Black pepper, and salt, as required
- Baguette or French bread slices
- Peanut butter, softened
- Garlic powder

Directions:

1. In a suitable-sized pot, melt the butter over medium heat.
2. Toss in the chopped onion and garlic mince to the pot. Sauté the onion for 5 minutes until transparent.
3. Add the broccoli florets to the pot and cook for a few minutes until they start to soften.
4. Pour in the vegetable broth and Cook the mixture to a boil. Reduce its heat and simmer for about 15 minutes until the broccoli is tender.
5. Use an immersion blender or transfer the soup to a blender to puree until smooth.
6. Return the pureed soup to the pot and stir in the grated cheddar cheese until melted and incorporated.
7. Stir in the low-fat cream. Season with black pepper, and salt, as required.
8. Meanwhile, preheat the oven to broil.
9. Spread peanut butter on one side of each bread slice and sprinkle with garlic powder.
10. Place the bread slices on a baking sheet and broil for a couple of minutes until the cheese is melted and golden.
11. Divide the broccoli and cheese soup into bowls and serve with the garlic cheese toasts on the side.

Nutritional Information (per serving): Calories: 290; Fat: 19.9g; Sodium: 330mg; Carbs: 10.5g; Fibers: 3g; Sugar: 3.6g; Proteins: 16.2g

130. Beef Carbonara

Prep time: 10 minutes. | **Cook time:** 20 minutes. |
Serves: 4

Ingredients:

- 8 oz. spaghetti
- 4 oz. lean ground beef
- 3 cloves garlic, minced
- 2 large eggs
- ½ cup low-fat cheddar cheese, grated
- Black pepper, and salt, as required
- Fresh parsley, chopped (for garnish)

Directions:

1. Cook the spaghetti as per package instructions until al dente. Drain once cooked then set it aside.
2. In a suitable-sized skillet, cook the ground beef over medium heat until browned and crispy. Remove it from the skillet with any slotted spoon and set aside.
3. In the same skillet, sauté the garlic mince until fragrant.
4. In a mixing bowl, mix the eggs and grated cheese.
5. Add the cooked spaghetti to the skillet with the garlic and toss to combine.
6. Pour the egg and cheese mixture over the spaghetti, tossing quickly to coat the pasta evenly. The heat of the pasta will cook the eggs.
7. Add the cooked beef and stir. Season with salt and black pepper to taste.
8. Cook for an extra minute to thoroughly heat everything.
9. Garnish the carbonara with fresh parsley while it is still hot and serve it. Enjoy

Nutritional Information (per serving): Calories: 413; Fat: 10.5g; Sodium: 734mg; Carbs: 32.4g; Fibers: 0.1g; Sugar: 0.2g; Proteins: 23.4g

131. Spaghetti with Meatballs and Cherry Tomatoes

Prep time: 10 minutes. | **Cook time:** 30 minutes. |
Serves: 6

Ingredients:

- 8 oz. spaghetti
- 1 lb. (ground) lean beef
- ½ cup breadcrumbs
- ¼ cup low-fat cheddar cheese, grated
- ¼ cup chopped fresh parsley
- 1 egg, beaten
- 2 cloves garlic, minced
- 1 teaspoon dried oregano
- ½ teaspoon salt
- ¼ teaspoon black pepper
- 2 tablespoons olive oil
- 1 pint cherry tomatoes
- 2 cups (low-sodium) Marinara sauce (to serve)
- Fresh basil leaves, torn (for garnish)

Directions:

1. Cook the spaghetti as per package instructions until al dente. Drain once cooked then set it aside.
2. In a suitable-sized bowl, mix the ground lean beef, breadcrumbs, cheddar cheese, chopped parsley, beaten egg, garlic mince, dried oregano, salt, and black pepper. Stir well until all of the ingredients are uniformly incorporated.
3. Shape the meat mixture into small meatballs, about 1 inch in diameter.
4. In a suitable-sized skillet, heat up the olive oil over medium heat. Add the meatballs to the skillet and cook for about 5-7 minutes, turning occasionally, until they are browned on all sides and cooked through.
5. Take the meatballs out of the skillet and put aside.
6. In the same skillet, add the cherry tomatoes and cook for 3-4 minutes until they start to soften and burst.
7. Return the meatballs to the skillet with the cherry tomatoes and pour in the marinara sauce. Stir everything and let it simmer for a few minutes to heat through.
8. Add the cooked spaghetti to the skillet and toss everything until the pasta is well coated with the sauce and meatballs.

9. Serve the spaghetti with meatballs and cherry tomatoes hot, garnished with torn fresh basil leaves.

Nutritional Information (per serving): Calories: 334; Fat: 13.3g; Sodium: 433mg; Carbs: 32.7g; Fibers: 1.4g; Sugar: 2.2g; Proteins: 23g

132. Brown Rice Salad with Borlotti Beans and Celery

Prep time: 40 minutes. | **Cook time:** 0 minutes. | **Serves:** 4

Ingredients:

- 1 cup cooked brown rice
- 1 can (15 oz.) borlotti beans, rinsed and drained
- 2 stalks celery, chopped
- ¼ cup chopped red onion
- ¼ cup chopped fresh parsley
- 2 tablespoons olive oil
- 2 tablespoons lemon juice
- 1 teaspoon Dijon mustard
- Black pepper, and salt, as required

Directions:

1. In a suitable-sized mixing bowl, mix the cooked brown rice, borlotti beans, chopped celery, red onion, and chopped parsley.
2. In a suitable-sized bowl, mix the olive oil, lemon juice, Dijon mustard, black pepper, and salt to make the dressing.
3. Pour the dressing over the rice and bean mixture. Toss everything until well coated.
4. Adjust the seasoning with more black pepper, and salt if needed.
5. Cover the bowl and refrigerate the salad for at least 30 minutes to allow the flavors to meld.
6. Serve the brown rice salad with borlotti beans and celery chilled, as a refreshing and nutritious side dish or light meal.

Nutritional Information (per serving): Calories: 301; Fat: 8.7g; Sodium: 27mg; Carbs: 48.8g; Fibers: 6g; Sugar: 0.8g; Proteins: 7.8g

133. Spiced Parsnip Soup

Prep time: 15 minutes. | **Cook time:** 25 minutes. | **Serves:** 4

Ingredients:

- 4 parsnips, peeled and chopped
- 1 onion, chopped
- 2 cloves garlic, minced
- 1 teaspoon (ground) cumin
- ½ teaspoon (ground) coriander
- ½ teaspoon (ground) turmeric
- ¼ teaspoon (ground) cinnamon
- 4 cups (low-sodium) vegetable broth
- 1 cup coconut milk
- 2 tablespoons olive oil
- Black pepper, and salt, as required
- Fresh cilantro, chopped (for garnish)

Directions:

1. In a suitable-sized pot, heat up the olive oil over medium heat. Toss in the chopped onion and garlic mince and sauté the onion for 5 minutes until translucent.
2. Toss in the chopped parsnips to the pot and cook for a few minutes until they start to soften.
3. Stir in the ground cumin, ground coriander, ground turmeric, and ground cinnamon. Cook for an additional minute to toast the spices and release their flavors.
4. Pour in the vegetable broth and Cook the mixture to a boil. Reduce its heat and simmer for about 15-20 minutes until the parsnips are tender.
5. Use an immersion blender or transfer the soup to a blender to puree until smooth.
6. Return the pureed soup to the pot and stir in the coconut milk. Season with black pepper, and salt, as required.
7. Simmer the soup for a few more minutes to heat through.
8. Serve the spiced parsnip soup hot, garnished with fresh chopped cilantro. Enjoy the comforting and flavorful soup.

Nutritional Information (per serving): Calories: 353; Fat: 23.3g; Sodium: 388mg; Carbs: 31.8g; Fibers: 8.7g; Sugar: 10.3g; Proteins: 8.3g

134. Creamy tuna and celery jacket potatoes

Prep time: 15 minutes. | **Cook time:** 1 hr. 15 minutes. | **Serves:** 4

Ingredients:

- 4 large baking potatoes
- 1 can of tuna, drained
- 2 celery stalks, finely chopped
- ¼ cup low-fat mayonnaise
- 2 tablespoons low-fat sour cream
- 2 tablespoons chopped fresh parsley
- 1 tablespoon lemon juice
- Black pepper, and salt, as required
- Optional toppings: grated cheese, sliced spring onions

Directions:

1. At 400°F (200°C), preheat your oven. Scrub the potatoes and pierce them several times with a fork. Place them directly on the oven rack and bake for about 1 hour.
2. While the potatoes are baking, prepare the tuna and celery filling. In a mixing bowl, mix the drained tuna, chopped celery, mayonnaise, sour cream, chopped parsley, and lemon juice. Stir until all the ingredients are evenly combined. Season to taste with black pepper, and salt.
3. Once the potatoes are cooked, remove them from the oven and allow them to cool slightly for a few minutes. Cut a lengthwise slit across the top of each potato, creating a pocket for the filling.
4. Spoon the tuna and celery mixture into each potato, dividing it equally among them. You can be generous with the filling, as the potatoes can hold a good amount.
5. If desired, sprinkle grated cheese on top of the filling. Return the potatoes to the oven and bake for an additional 10-15 minutes.
6. Take the potatoes out of the oven and let them cool for a few minutes. Garnish with sliced spring onions and additional chopped parsley.

Nutritional Information (per serving): Calories: 284; Fat: 10.1g; Sodium: 156mg; Carbs: 34.6g; Fibers: 2.6g; Sugar: 2.3g; Proteins: 15.8g

135. Celeriac and White Bean Soup

Prep time: 10 minutes. | **Cook time:** 25 minutes. | **Serves:** 4

Ingredients:

- 1 large celeriac, peeled and diced
- 1 onion, chopped
- 2 cloves garlic, minced
- 2 tablespoons olive oil
- 1 can (15 oz.) white beans, drained and rinsed
- 4 cups (low-sodium) vegetable broth
- Black pepper, and salt, as required
- **For the Glazed Apple:**
- 1 apple, cored and thinly sliced
- 1 tablespoon peanut butter
- 1 tablespoon honey
- Fresh parsley, chopped (for garnish)

Directions:

1. In a suitable-sized pot, heat up the olive oil over medium heat. Toss in the chopped onion and garlic mince and sauté the onion for 5 minutes until translucent.
2. Toss in the diced celeriac to the pot and cook for a few minutes until it starts to soften.
3. Pour in the vegetable broth and Cook the mixture to a boil. Reduce its heat and simmer for about 20-25 minutes until the celeriac is tender.
4. Use an immersion blender or transfer the soup to a blender to puree until smooth.
5. Return the pureed soup to the pot and stir in the white beans. Season with black pepper, and salt, as required.
6. In a separate skillet, melt the butter over medium heat. Add the apple slices and cook until they start to soften.
7. Drizzle the honey over the apple slices and cook for an additional minute until they are glazed and caramelized.
8. Divide the celeriac and white bean soup into bowls. Top each bowl with glazed apple slices, and chopped fresh parsley.
9. Serve the soup warm and enjoy the combination of flavors and textures.

Nutritional Information (per serving): Calories: 391; Fat: 22.6g; Sodium: 375mg; Carbs: 32g; Fibers: 7.5g; Sugar: 12.8g; Proteins: 16.6g

136. Ricotta Dumplings with Orecchiette, and Peas

Nutritional Information (per serving): Calories: 412; Fat: 13.2g; Sodium: 408mg; Carbs: 37.7g; Fibers: 3.6g; Sugar: 3.6g; Proteins: 34.6g

Prep time: 15 minutes.| **Cook time:** 20 minutes.| **Serves:** 4

Ingredients:

- 8 oz. orecchiette pasta
- 1 cup frozen peas
- Low-fat parmesan cheese, grated (for serving)
- Fresh basil leaves, torn (for garnish)
- **For the Ricotta Dumplings:**
- 1 cup ricotta cheese
- ¼ cup low-fat cheddar cheese, grated
- ¼ cup breadcrumbs
- ¼ cup chopped fresh parsley
- 1 egg, lightly beaten
- ¼ teaspoon black pepper

Directions:

1. In a suitable-sized pot, cook the orecchiette pasta as per package instructions until al dente. During the last few minutes of cooking, add the frozen peas to the boiling water. Drain the pasta and peas, reserving a small amount of the cooking water.
2. In a mixing bowl, mix the ricotta cheese, grated cheese, breadcrumbs, chopped parsley, beaten egg, salt, and black pepper. Stir well until all of the ingredients are uniformly incorporated.
3. Roll the ricotta mixture into small dumplings, about 1 inch in diameter.
4. In the same pot used for cooking the pasta, heat a little olive oil over medium heat. Add the ricotta dumplings to the pot and cook for about 3-4 minutes until they are lightly browned on all sides. Remove the dumplings from the pot and set aside.
5. Return the cooked pasta and peas to the pot. Stir everything together, adding a little bit of the reserved cooking water if needed to loosen the sauce.
6. Serve the orecchiette pasta with ricotta dumplings, and peas in bowls. Sprinkle with freshly grated Parmesan cheese and torn fresh basil leaves.
7. Enjoy the delicious ricotta dumplings with the combination of flavors from the peas, and Parmesan cheese.

Smoothies & Mocktails

137. Iced Banana Turmeric Smoothie

Prep time: 5 minutes. | **Cook time:** 0 minutes. | **Serves:** 2

Ingredients:

- 2 ripe bananas, peeled and frozen
- 1 cup almond milk
- 1 teaspoon (ground) turmeric
- 1 tablespoon honey (for added sweetness)

Directions:

1. Place the frozen bananas, almond milk, ground turmeric, and honey in a blender.
2. Blend on high speed until all the ingredients are well combined and you have a smooth and creamy consistency.
3. Pour the smoothie into a glass, then serve right away.
4. Enjoy the iced banana turmeric smoothie as a refreshing and nutritious drink.

Nutritional Information (per serving): Calories: 417; Fat: 29.1g; Sodium: 20mg; Carbs: 43g; Fibers: 6g; Sugar: 27.1g; Proteins: 4.2g

138. Berry Smoothie with Spinach

Prep time: 5 minutes. | **Cook time:** 0 minutes. | **Serves:** 2

Ingredients:

- 1 cup mixed berries (strawberries, blueberries, and raspberries), fresh or frozen
- 1 ripe banana
- 1 cup spinach leaves
- 1 cup almond milk
- Optional: 1 tablespoon honey

Directions:

1. Place the mixed berries, banana, spinach leaves, almond milk, and honey in a blender.
2. Blend on high speed until all the ingredients are well combined and you have a smooth and vibrant purple smoothie.
3. Pour the smoothie into a glass, then serve right away.
4. Enjoy the berry smoothie with spinach as a delicious and nutrient-packed way to start your day.

Nutritional Information (per serving): Calories: 108; Fat: 1g; Sodium: 40mg; Carbs: 24.1g; Fibers: 4.4g; Sugar: 13.5g; Proteins: 1.8g

139. Turmeric, Ginger, and Apple Spice Smoothie

Prep time: 5 minutes. | **Cook time:** 0 minutes. | **Serves:** 2

Ingredients:

- 1 apple, cored and chopped
- 1 ripe banana
- 1 cup almond milk
- ½ teaspoon (ground) turmeric
- ½ teaspoon (ground) ginger
- ¼ teaspoon (ground) cinnamon
- Optional: 1 tablespoon honey

Directions:

1. Place the chopped apple, banana, almond milk, ground turmeric, ground ginger, ground cinnamon, and honey in a blender.
2. Blend on high speed until all the ingredients are well combined and you have a smooth and flavorful smoothie.
3. Pour the smoothie into a glass, then serve right away.
4. Enjoy the turmeric, ginger, and apple spice smoothie as a warming and immune-boosting beverage.

Nutritional Information (per serving): Calories: 391; Fat: 29.1g; Sodium: 20mg; Carbs: 36.4g; Fibers: 7.2g; Sugar: 22.9g; Proteins: 3.8g

140. Blueberry Coconut Smoothie

Prep time: 5 minutes. | **Cook time:** 0 minutes. | **Serves:** 1

Ingredients:

- 1 cup blueberries, fresh or frozen
- 1 ripe banana
- ½ cup coconut milk
- ½ cup Greek yogurt (or dairy-free alternative)
- Optional: 1 tablespoon honey

Directions:

1. Place the blueberries, banana, coconut milk, Greek yogurt, and honey in a blender.
2. Blend on high speed until all the ingredients are well combined and you have a smooth and creamy purple smoothie.
3. Pour the smoothie into a glass, then serve right away.
4. Enjoy the blueberry coconut smoothie as a delicious and nutritious treat.

Nutritional Information (per serving): Calories: 539; Fat: 31.5g; Sodium: 53mg; Carbs: 58.6g; Fibers: 9.2g; Sugar: 36.8g; Proteins: 15.1g

141. Spa Smoothie

Prep time: 5 minutes. | **Cook time:** 0 minutes. | **Serves:** 4

Ingredients:

- 1 cucumber, peeled and chopped
- 1 cup spinach leaves
- 1 cup pineapple chunks
- ½ cup coconut water
- Juice of 1 lime
- Optional: Fresh mint leaves (for garnish)

Directions:

1. Place the cucumber, spinach leaves, pineapple chunks, coconut water, and lime juice in a blender.
2. Blend on high speed until all the ingredients are well combined and you have a refreshing and vibrant green smoothie.
3. Pour the smoothie into a glass and garnish with mint leaves.

4. Serve the spa smoothie immediately and enjoy it's refreshing and detoxifying properties.

Nutritional Information (per serving): Calories: 157; Fat: 0.9g; Sodium: 158mg; Carbs: 38.1g; Fibers: 5.8g; Sugar: 24.5g; Proteins: 4.6g

142. Healthy Beet Cocktail

Prep time: 5 minutes. | **Cook time:** 0 minutes. | **Serves:** 1

Ingredients:

- 1 medium-sized beet, cooked and peeled
- 1 apple, cored and chopped
- 1 carrot, peeled and chopped
- Juice of 1 lemon
- 1-inch piece of ginger, peeled
- Optional: Honey

Directions:

1. Place the cooked beet, apple, carrot, lemon juice, and ginger in a blender.
2. Blend on high speed until all the ingredients are well combined and you have a nutrient-packed cocktail.
3. Taste the mixture and if desired, add honey for added sweetness. Blend again to incorporate.
4. Pour the healthy beet cocktail into a glass and serve immediately.
5. Enjoy the beet cocktail as a refreshing and invigorating drink, rich in antioxidants and vitamins.

Nutritional Information (per serving): Calories: 178; Fat: 0.6g; Sodium: 109mg; Carbs: 45.3g; Fibers: 8.6g; Sugar: 33g; Proteins: 2.5g

143. Strawberry Water

Prep time: 5 minutes. | **Cook time:** 0 minutes. | **Serves:** 1

Ingredients:

- 1 cup strawberries, hulled and sliced
- 4 cups water
- Optional: Mint leaves or lemon slices (for added flavor)

Directions:

1. In a pitcher, mix the sliced strawberries and water.
2. Optional: Add a few fresh mint leaves or lemon slices to enhance the flavor.
3. Mix well and let the mixture sit in the refrigerator for at least 1 hour to infuse the water with the strawberry flavor.
4. Serve the refreshing strawberry water over ice and garnish with additional strawberry slices or mint leaves.
5. Enjoy the light and fruity strawberry-infused water as a hydrating and flavorful beverage.

Nutritional Information (per serving): Calories: 46; Fat: 0.4g; Sodium: 30mg; Carbs: 11.1g; Fibers: 2.9g; Sugar: 7.1g; Proteins: 1g

144. Celery Smoothie

Prep time: 5 minutes. | **Cook time:** 0 minutes. | **Serves:** 1

Ingredients:

- 2 stalks celery, chopped
- 1 green apple, cored and chopped
- 1 ripe banana
- 1 cup spinach leaves
- 1 cup almond milk
- Optional: 1 tablespoon honey

Directions:

1. Place the celery, green apple, banana, spinach leaves, almond milk, and honey in a blender.
2. Blend on high speed until all the ingredients are well combined and you have a smooth and vibrant green smoothie.
3. Pour the smoothie into a glass, then serve right away.
4. Enjoy the celery smoothie as a refreshing and nutrient-packed drink.

Nutritional Information (per serving): Calories: 293; Fat: 3.5g; Sodium: 194mg; Carbs: 67.9g; Fibers: 9.7g; Sugar: 44.2g; Proteins: 4g

145. Skinny Party Punch

Prep time: 5 minutes. | **Cook time:** 0 minutes. | **Serves:** 16 (1 gallon)

Ingredients:

- 4 cups pineapple juice
- 4 cups diet cranberry juice
- 2 liters diet ginger ale

Directions:

1. Combine pineapple juice and diet cranberry juice, then stir in ginger ale just prior to serving.
2. Enjoy.

Nutritional Information (per serving): Calories: 41; Fat: 0.1g; Sodium: 11mg; Carbs: 10.1g; Fiber 0.1g; Sugars 8.5g; Protein 0.2g

146. Sugarless Mojito

Prep time: 5 minutes. | **Cook time:** 0 minutes. | **Serves:** 1

Ingredients:

- 1 lime, cut into wedges
- 8-10 fresh mint leaves
- Sparkling water
- Ice cubes
- Optional: Stevia or any sugar substitute

Directions:

1. In a glass, muddle the lime wedges and mint leaves using a muddler or the back of a spoon. This will release the flavors and aromas.
2. Fill the glass with ice cubes.
3. Pour sparkling water into the glass, filling it to the top.
4. Optional: If desired, add a small amount of stevia or any sugar substitute to sweeten the mojito. Adjust the amount according to your preference.
5. Mix well to combine all the ingredients.
6. Garnish with a sprig of fresh mint leaves.
7. Serve the sugarless mojito immediately and enjoy the refreshing and zesty flavors.

Nutritional Information (per serving): Calories: 40; Fat: 0.7g; Sodium: 30mg; Carbs: 7.7g; Fibers: 6.2g; Sugar: 0g; Proteins: 3g

Gluten Free Dishes

147. Sheet Pan Chickpea Chicken

Prep time: 10 minutes. | **Cook time:** 25 minutes. | **Serves:** 4

Ingredients:

- 4 boneless, skinless chicken breasts
- 1 can (15 oz.) chickpeas, drained and rinsed
- 1 red bell pepper, sliced
- 1 yellow bell pepper, sliced
- 1 red onion, sliced
- 2 tablespoons olive oil
- 1 teaspoon paprika
- 1 teaspoon (ground) cumin
- ½ teaspoon garlic powder
- ½ teaspoon salt
- ¼ teaspoon black pepper
- Fresh parsley, chopped (for garnish)

Directions:

1. At 425°F (220°C), preheat your oven
2. In a suitable-sized bowl, mix the chickpeas, bell peppers, red onion, olive oil, paprika, ground cumin, garlic powder, salt, and black pepper. Toss well to coat everything in the spices and oil.
3. Place the chicken breasts on a baking sheet and arrange the seasoned chickpeas, bell peppers, and onion around the chicken.
4. Roast the sheet pan chickpea chicken in the oven for 20-25 minutes.
5. Remove from the oven and let the chicken rest for a few minutes before slicing.
6. Garnish with chopped parsley and serve the roasted chicken with the seasoned chickpeas, bell peppers, and onion.

Nutritional Information (per serving): Calories: 419; Fat: 18.7g; Sodium: 417mg; Carbs: 16.9g; Fibers: 4.4g; Sugar: 4.8g; Proteins: 45g

148. Chickpea, Spinach, and Quinoa Patties

Prep time: 10 minutes. | **Cook time:** 10 minutes. | **Serves:** 2

Ingredients:

- 1 can (15 oz.) chickpeas, drained and rinsed
- 1 cup cooked quinoa
- 1 cup fresh spinach, chopped
- ¼ cup low-fat parmesan cheese, grated
- ¼ cup bread crumbs
- ¼ cup finely chopped onion
- 2 cloves garlic, minced
- 1 teaspoon (ground) cumin
- ½ teaspoon paprika
- ½ teaspoon salt
- ¼ teaspoon black pepper
- 2 eggs, beaten
- 2 tablespoons olive oil

Directions:

1. In a suitable-sized bowl, mash the chickpeas with a fork until they are partially mashed but still have some texture.
2. Add the cooked quinoa, chopped spinach, Parmesan cheese, bread crumbs, onion, garlic, ground cumin, paprika, salt, black pepper, and beaten eggs to the bowl. Mix well until all ingredients are combined.
3. Shape the mixture into patties, approximately 2-3 inches in diameter.
4. Heat up the olive oil in a suitable-sized skillet over medium heat.
5. Cook the chickpea, spinach, and quinoa patties in the skillet for 3-4 minutes per side.
6. Remove the patties from the skillet and place them on a paper towel-lined plate to drain any excess oil.
7. Serve the chickpea, spinach, and quinoa patties as a vegetarian burger in a bun with your favorite toppings or as a side dish with a salad or roasted vegetables.

Nutritional Information (per serving): Calories: 393; Fat: 10.4g; Sodium: 802mg; Carbs: 56g; Fibers: 10.4g; Sugar: 5.9g; Proteins: 20.8g

149. Roasted Squash, Pork, and Kale Salad With Cherries

Prep time: 15 minutes. | **Cook time:** 45 minutes. | Serves: 4

Ingredients:

- 1 small butternut squash, peeled, seeded, and cut into 1-inch cubes
- 1 tablespoon olive oil
- Black pepper, and salt, as required
- 1 lb. pork tenderloin, trimmed
- 1 tablespoon smoked paprika
- 4 cups kale, stems removed and leaves torn into bite-sized pieces
- 1 cup fresh cherries, pitted and halved
- ¼ cup crumbled feta cheese
- ¼ cup chopped walnuts
- 2 tablespoons balsamic vinegar
- 2 tablespoons extra-virgin olive oil

Directions:

1. At 400°F (200°C), preheat your oven.
2. Place the butternut squash cubes on a baking sheet. Drizzle olive oil and season with black pepper, and salt. Toss to coat the squash evenly. Roast for 20-25 minutes in a preheated oven. Set aside.
3. Meanwhile, season the pork tenderloin with smoked paprika, black pepper, and salt. Heat a skillet over medium-high heat and add a drizzle of olive oil. Sear the pork tenderloin on all sides until browned, then transfer it to a baking dish. Roast in the oven for about 15-20 minutes.
4. Remove from the oven and let it rest for a few minutes before slicing into thin rounds.
5. In a suitable-sized bowl, mix the kale, roasted butternut squash, sliced pork, cherries, feta cheese, and chopped walnuts.
6. In a suitable-sized bowl, mix the balsamic vinegar and extra-virgin olive oil. Drizzle the prepared dressing over the salad and toss to combine.
7. Serve the salad immediately as a main course or divide into individual plates.
8. Enjoy the delicious and nutritious roasted squash, pork, and kale salad with cherries!

Nutritional Information (per serving): Calories: 342; Fat: 14.4g; Sodium: 204mg; Carbs: 18.5g; Fibers: 3g; Sugar: 1.5g; Proteins: 35.6g

150. Smoked Paprika Steak and Lentils with Spinach

Prep time: 10 minutes. | **Cook time:** 40 minutes. | Serves: 2

Ingredients:

- 2 boneless ribeye steaks
- 2 teaspoons smoked paprika
- Black pepper, and salt, as required
- 1 cup dried green lentils
- 3 cups water
- 2 tablespoons olive oil
- 3 cloves garlic, minced
- 4 cups fresh spinach leaves
- 1 lemon, zest and juice

Directions:

1. Preheat a grill or grill pan over medium-high heat.
2. Season the steaks with smoked paprika, black pepper, and salt on both sides. Grill the steaks for about 4-6 minutes per side for medium-rare. Remove the steaks from the grill and let them rest for a few minutes before slicing.
3. While the steaks are grilling, rinse the lentils under cold water and drain. In a medium saucepan, mix the lentils and water. Bring to a boil, then reduce its heat to low and simmer for about 20-25 minutes. Drain any excess liquid and set aside.
4. Heat olive oil in a suitable-sized skillet over medium heat. Add garlic mince and cook for about 1 minute until fragrant.
5. Add the cooked lentils to the skillet with garlic and toss to coat. Cook for an additional 2-3 minutes to heat through.
6. Add the spinach leaves to the skillet and cook until wilted, stir occasionally.
7. Remove the skillet from heat and squeeze fresh lemon juice over the lentils and spinach. Add the lemon zest and season with black pepper, and salt, as required. Stir to combine.
8. Slice the grilled steaks and serve them on top of the lentils and spinach mixture.
9. Garnish with additional lemon zest if desired and serve the smoked paprika steak and lentils with spinach hot. Enjoy this delicious dish!

Nutritional Information (per serving): Calories: 488; Fat: 15.6g; Sodium: 66mg; Carbs: 62.6g; Fibers: 31.5g; Sugar: 2.5g; Proteins: 27.4g

151. Sesame Chicken

Prep time: 1 hr. 10 minutes. | **Cook time:** 10 minutes. | **Serves:** 2

Nutritional Information (per serving): Calories: 536; Fat: 30.9g; Sodium: 431mg; Carbs: 19.5g; Fibers: 2.2g; Sugar: 9.7g; Proteins: 44g

Ingredients:

- For the chicken marinade:
- 1.5 lbs. boneless, skinless chicken breasts, cut into bite-sized pieces
- 2 tablespoons (low-sodium) soy sauce
- 1 tablespoon honey
- 1 tablespoon rice vinegar
- 1 teaspoon sesame oil
- 2 cloves garlic, minced
- 1 teaspoon grated fresh ginger
- **For the sauce:**
- 2 tablespoons (low-sodium) soy sauce
- 1 tablespoon honey
- 1 tablespoon rice vinegar
- 1 teaspoon sesame oil
- 1 tablespoon cornstarch
- ¼ cup water
- **For cooking:**
- 2 tablespoons vegetable oil
- 2 tablespoons sesame seeds
- 4 green onion-s, sliced

Directions:

1. In a bowl, combine all the marinade ingredients soy sauce, honey, rice vinegar, sesame oil, garlic mince, and grated ginger. Add the chicken pieces and toss to coat. Let the chicken marinate for at least 15 minutes, or chill for up to an hour for extra flavor.
2. In a separate bowl, mix the soy sauce, honey, rice vinegar, sesame oil, cornstarch, and water to make the sauce. Set it aside.
3. Heat vegetable oil in a suitable-sized skillet or wok over medium-high heat. Add the marinated chicken pieces and cook for about 5-7 minutes.
4. Pour the sauce over the cooked chicken in the skillet. Mix well to coat the chicken evenly with the sauce. Continue cooking for an additional 2-3 minutes.
5. If desired, roast the sesame seeds in a dry skillet over medium heat until golden brown.
6. Serve the sesame chicken over steamed rice or noodles. Sesame seeds and sliced green onions can be added as garnish.
7. Enjoy the delicious and savory sesame chicken!

Air Fryer Dishes

152. Buffalo Cauliflower

Prep time: 15 minutes. | **Cook time:** 18 minutes. | Serves: 2

Ingredients:

- 1 head of cauliflower, cut into florets
- ½ cup whole-wheat flour
- ½ cup coconut milk
- 1 teaspoon garlic powder
- 1 teaspoon onion powder
- ½ teaspoon paprika
- ¼ teaspoon black pepper
- ½ cup buffalo sauce
- Cooking spray

Directions:

1. At 400°F (200°C), preheat your air fryer.
2. In a bowl, mix the flour, milk, garlic powder, onion powder, paprika, salt, and black pepper until you have a smooth batter.
3. Dip each cauliflower floret into the prepared batter, making sure it's fully coated, and allow any excess batter to drip off.
4. Lightly grease the air fryer basket with cooking spray to prevent sticking.
5. Place the coated cauliflower florets in a single layer in the air fryer basket. You may need to work in batches depending on the size of your air fryer.
6. Cook the cauliflower in the air fryer for 15-18 minutes, flip halfway through, until they are golden brown and crispy.
7. Remove the cauliflower from the air fryer and place it in a clean bowl. Drizzle the buffalo sauce over the cauliflower and toss gently to coat.
8. Serve the air fryer buffalo cauliflower with your favorite dipping sauce or alongside celery sticks and ranch dressing.

Nutritional Information (per serving): Calories: 195; Fat: 1.8g; Sodium: 432mg; Carbs: 37.3g; Fibers: 5.1g; Sugar: 6.8g; Proteins: 8.3g

153. Chicken Tenders

Prep time: 10 minutes. | **Cook time:** 15 minutes. | Serves: 2

Ingredients:

- 1 lb. chicken tenders
- 1 cup bread crumbs
- ¼ cup low-fat parmesan cheese, grated
- 1 teaspoon paprika
- ½ teaspoon garlic powder
- ½ teaspoon onion powder
- ¼ teaspoon black pepper
- 2 large eggs, beaten
- Cooking spray

Directions:

1. At 400°F (200°C), preheat your air fryer.
2. In any right-sized shallow dish, mix the bread crumbs, Parmesan cheese, paprika, garlic powder, onion powder, salt, and black pepper.
3. Dip each chicken tender into the beaten eggs, allowing any excess to drip off.
4. Coat the chicken tender in the bread crumb mixture, pressing it gently to adhere.
5. Lightly grease the air fryer basket with cooking spray.
6. Place the coated chicken tenders in a single layer in the air fryer basket. You may need to work in batches depending on the size of your air fryer.
7. Spray the tops of the chicken tenders with cooking spray to promote browning.
8. Cook the chicken tenders in the air fryer for 10-12 minutes, flip halfway through, until they are golden brown and cooked through.
9. Serve the air fryer chicken tenders with your favorite dipping sauce, barbecue sauce, honey mustard, or ranch dressing.

Nutritional Information (per serving): Calories: 570; Fat: 19.1g; Sodium: 401mg; Carbs: 41.1g; Fibers: 3g; Sugar: 4.2g; Proteins: 55.5g

154. Air-Fried Meatballs

Prep time: 10 minutes. | **Cook time:** 15 minutes. |
Serves: 4

Ingredients:

- 1 lb. (ground) lean beef
- ½ cup bread crumbs
- ¼ cup low-fat parmesan cheese, grated
- ¼ cup chopped fresh parsley
- 1 teaspoon garlic powder
- 1 teaspoon onion powder
- ½ teaspoon salt
- ¼ teaspoon black pepper
- 1 large egg, beaten
- Cooking spray

Directions:

1. At 400°F (200°C), preheat your air fryer.
2. In a suitable-sized bowl, mix the (ground) lean beef, bread crumbs, Parmesan cheese, parsley, garlic powder, onion powder, salt, black pepper, and beaten egg. Stir until all components are evenly incorporated.
3. Form the mixture into small meatballs about an inch in diameter.
4. Spray the air fryer basket lightly with cooking spray.
5. Place the meatballs in a single layer in the air fryer basket. You may need to work in batches depending on the size of your air fryer.
6. Spray the tops of the meatballs with cooking spray to promote browning.
7. Cook the meatballs in the air fryer for 12-15 minutes, shaking the basket or flip the meatballs halfway through, until they are browned and cooked through.
8. Remove the meatballs from the air fryer and let them cool slightly before serving.
9. Serve the air-fried meatballs as an appetizer with your favorite dipping sauce or as a main dish with pasta, rice, or on sub rolls for meatball sandwiches.

Nutritional Information (per serving): Calories: 258; Fat: 8.8g; Sodium: 531mg; Carbs: 11.4g; Fibers: 0.9g; Sugar: 1.4g; Proteins: 31.7g

155. Baked Potato

Prep time: 10 minutes. | **Cook time:** 40 minutes. |
Serves: 4

Ingredients:

- 4 medium-sized Russet potatoes
- 1 tablespoon olive oil
- Salt, to taste
- Toppings of your choice (e.g., sour cream, grated cheese, chives)

Directions:

1. At 400°F (200°C), preheat your air fryer.
2. Scrub the potatoes clean and dry them thoroughly.
3. Poke each potato several times with a fork to create small holes for steam to escape during cooking.
4. Rub the potatoes with olive oil, ensuring they are evenly coated.
5. Sprinkle salt over the oiled potatoes.
6. Place the potatoes in a single layer in the air fryer basket. You may need to work in batches depending on the size of your air fryer.
7. Cook the potatoes in the air fryer for 35-40 minutes, flip them halfway through until they are tender and the skins are crispy.
8. Once the potatoes are cooked, remove them from the air fryer and let them cool for a few minutes.
9. Cut a slit in the top of each potato and fluff the insides with a fork.
10. Add your favorite toppings, sour cream, grated cheese, and chives.
11. Serve the air fryer baked potatoes as a side dish or as a main course with additional toppings and a side salad.

Nutritional Information (per serving): Calories: 177; Fat: 3.7g; Sodium: 52mg; Carbs: 33.5g; Fibers: 5.1g; Sugar: 2.5g; Proteins: 3.6g

156. Rotisserie Roasted Whole Chicken

Prep time: 10 minutes. | **Cook time:** 50 minutes. |
Serves: 8

Ingredients:

- 1 whole chicken (4 lbs.)
- 2 tablespoons olive oil
- 1 tablespoon paprika
- 1 teaspoon garlic powder
- 1 teaspoon onion powder
- 1 teaspoon dried thyme
- ½ teaspoon black pepper

Directions:

1. At 375°F (190°C), preheat your air fryer.
2. Pat the whole chicken dry with paper towels.
3. In a suitable-sized bowl, mix the olive oil, paprika, garlic powder, onion powder, dried thyme, salt, and black pepper to create a spice rub.
4. Rub the spice mixture all over the chicken, ensuring it is evenly coated.
5. Place the chicken breast-side down in the air fryer basket.
6. Cook the chicken in the air fryer for 25 minutes.
7. Carefully flip the chicken and continue cooking for an additional 25 minutes.
8. Using a meat thermometer, determine the chicken's internal temperature. It should read 165°F (74°C) in the thickest part of the thigh without touching the bone.
9. If the chicken has not reached the desired temperature, continue cooking in 5-minute increments until done.
10. Once the chicken is fully cooked, remove it from the air fryer and let it rest for 10 minutes before carving.
11. Carve the air fryer rotisserie roasted whole chicken and serve it with your favorite side dishes, roasted vegetables, mashed potatoes, or a fresh salad.

Nutritional Information (per serving): Calories: 348; Fat: 18.1g; Sodium: 408mg; Carbs: 2.3g; Fibers: 0.9g; Sugar: 0.6g; Proteins: 42.7g

8 Weeks Meal Plans

Meal Planning and Prep

It always helps when you plan and prepare your meals in advance. By assigning time to carefully plan meals ahead of time, you get to enjoy all the nutritious meals, and you minimize the chances of consuming unhealthy foods due to limitation of time. Meal planning helps to intentionally select all the heart-healthy ingredients. By cooking meals at home, you can have better control over your portion sizes and cooking methods, which helps to maintain calorie intake and reduce the risk of weight gain.

Meal Prep Tips

Good and effective meal-prepping techniques can make a diet more manageable for busy individuals. Here are some recommendations to help you prepare heart-healthy meals in advance:

Try cooking in batches: Spare a day or two each week to cook all the meals in batches. Cook larger portions of dishes that can be easily reheated or reused throughout the week. For example, you can cook a large batch of rice, quinoa, or roasted vegetables that can be stored and served as a base for multiple meals.

Use the freezer to store food: Many heart-healthy dishes can be frozen for later use. Cook extra servings of soups, stews, or casseroles and freeze them in individual or family-sized portions. This way, you will have healthy meals readily available when you are short on time.

Prepare your ingredients in advance: Take the time to chop vegetables, wash and dry salad greens, and prepare other ingredients in advance. Store them in airtight containers or bags in the refrigerator so that they are ready to use when it's time to cook.

Keep mason jar salads: Use mason jars to layer and pack your salads in advance. Start with the dressing at the bottom, followed by hearty vegetables, proteins, grains, and finally, the leafy greens on top. When you are ready to eat, simply mix salads in the jar to distribute the dressing, then serve.

Prefer portion control: Divide the prepared meals into single portions to ensure you are not overeating. Use portion control containers or divide your meals into single-serving meal prep containers.

Grab-and-go snacks: Prepare healthy snacks ahead of time to avoid consuming unhealthy options when hunger strikes. Slice your favorite fruits and vegetables, use nuts and seeds, or make homemade energy balls or protein bars to eat as healthy snacks.

Keep it simple: Remember that not every meal needs to be fancy on your weekly menu. Simple and easy-to-make meals can be just as nutritious and time-saving. Consider making healthy salads with pre-washed greens, canned beans, and grilled chicken or fish for a quick and healthy option.

Week 01

Days	Breakfast	Lunch	Snack	Dinner	Dessert
Monday	Everything bagel avocado toast	Lemon-garlic steak & green beans	Homemade multi-seed crackers	Lentil & vegetable soup with parmesan	Banana mousse
Tuesday	Banana chocolate chip mini muffins	Skillet steak with mushroom sauce	Mini bell pepper pebre	Sweet potato & bean enchiladas	Chocolate bark with espresso and toasted nuts
Wednesday	Two-ingredient banana pancakes	Baked beans with ground lean beef	Pimiento cheese-stuffed mini bell peppers	Crispy egg noodles with tofu & peanut sauce	Dark chocolate frozen banana bites
Thursday	Breakfast beans with microwave-poached egg	Balsamic pork tenderloin	Radishes with green goddess dressing	Seitan bbq sandwiches	Blueberry gratin
Friday	Southwestern waffles	Sesame-garlic beef & broccoli with whole-wheat noodles	Baked parsnip chips	Zucchini-chickpea veggie burgers with tahini-ranch sauce	Buckwheat crepes
Saturday	Pistachio & peach toast	Lamb chops with mint pan sauce	Baked zucchini waffle fries with creamy herb dip	Lemon-pepper linguine with squash	Caramelized pineapple with raspberries
Sunday	Sweet potato kale breakfast salad	Chicken kebabs	Chili-lime brussels sprout chips	Mushroom shawarma with yogurt-tahini sauce	Raspberry banana sorbet

Week 02

Days	Breakfast	Lunch	Snack	Dinner	Dessert
Monday	Egg tartine	Grilled mahi-mahi	Grilled chicken and cherry salad	Grain bowl with chickpeas & cauliflower	Chia pudding
Tuesday	Cannellini bean & herbed ricotta toast	Red pepper & parmesan tilapia	Fresh taco salad	Roasted vegetable bowls with pesto	Dark chocolate and cherry brownies
Wednesday	Creamy blueberry-pecan oatmeal	Chimichurri baked flounder	Shrimp and rice noodle salad	Stuffed sweet potato with hummus dressing	Avocado brownies
Thursday	Everything bagel avocado toast	Grilled halibut with blueberry salsa	Indian garbanzo bean salad with pitas	Veggie & hummus sandwich	Banana mousse
Friday	Banana chocolate chip mini muffins	Walnut and oat-crusted salmon	Maple mahi-mahi salad	Roasted vegetable & black bean tacos	Chocolate bark with espresso and toasted nuts
Saturday	Two-ingredient banana pancakes	Grilled blackened shrimp tacos	Stone fruit salad with baked goat cheese coins	Mushroom & tofu stir-fry	Dark chocolate frozen banana bites
Sunday	Breakfast beans with microwave-poached egg	Green curry salmon with green beans	Wilted spinach salad with pears and cranberries	Roasted root veggies & greens over spiced lentils	Blueberry gratin

Week 03

Days	Breakfast	Lunch	Snack	Dinner	Dessert
Monday	Southwestern waffles	Chicken, brussels sprouts & mushrooms one-pot pasta	Homemade multi-seed crackers	Honey glazed salmon	Banana mousse
Tuesday	Pistachio & peach toast	Honey-roasted chicken thighs with sweet potato wedges	Mini bell pepper pebre	Bean burger	Chocolate bark with espresso and toasted nuts
Wednesday	Sweet potato kale breakfast salad	Slow-cooked ranch chicken and vegetables	Pimiento cheese-stuffed mini bell peppers	Grilled shrimp	Dark chocolate frozen banana bites
Thursday	Egg tartine	Skillet lemon chicken & potatoes with kale	Radishes with green goddess dressing	Chicken kebabs	Blueberry gratin
Friday	Cannellini bean & herbed ricotta toast	Garlic cashew chicken casserole	Baked parsnip chips	Pan-seared steak with crispy herbs & escarole	Buckwheat crepes
Saturday	Creamy blueberry-pecan oatmeal	Roast chicken & sweet potatoes	Baked zucchini waffle fries with creamy herb dip	Mushroom & tofu stir-fry	Caramelized pineapple with raspberries
Sunday	Everything bagel avocado toast	Beef stir-fry with baby bok choy & ginger	Chili-lime brussels sprout chips	Easy pea & spinach carbonara	Raspberry banana sorbet

Week 04

Days	Breakfast	Lunch	Snack	Dinner	Dessert
Monday	Banana chocolate chip mini muffins	Healthy baked halibut	Grilled chicken and cherry salad	Grilled salmon with cilantro-ginger sauce	Chia pudding
Tuesday	Two-ingredient banana pancakes	Steamed tilapia in wine sauce	Fresh taco salad	One-pot garlicky shrimp & spinach	Dark chocolate and cherry brownies
Wednesday	Breakfast beans with microwave-poached egg	Miso-maple salmon	Shrimp and rice noodle salad	Farfalle with mushrooms and spinach	Avocado brownies
Thursday	Egg tartine	Charred shrimp & pesto buddha bowls	Indian garbanzo bean salad with pitas	Thai chicken risotto	Banana mousse
Friday	Cannellini bean & herbed ricotta toast	Roasted salmon with sautéed balsamic spinach	Maple mahi-mahi salad	Roasted sweet potatoes with chili and seeds	Chocolate bark with espresso and toasted nuts
Saturday	Creamy blueberry-pecan oatmeal	Crumb-coated red snapper	Stone fruit salad with baked goat cheese coins	Prawn and spinach angel hair pasta with prawn oil	Dark chocolate frozen banana bites
Sunday	Everything bagel avocado toast	Halibut soft tacos	Wilted spinach salad with pears and cranberries	Beef spaghetti	Blueberry gratin

Week 05

Days	Breakfast	Lunch	Snack	Dinner	Dessert
Monday	Everything bagel avocado toast	Lemon-garlic steak & green beans	Homemade multi-seed crackers	Lentil & vegetable soup with parmesan	Banana mousse
Tuesday	Banana chocolate chip mini muffins	Skillet steak with mushroom sauce	Mini bell pepper pebre	Sweet potato & bean enchiladas	Chocolate bark with espresso and toasted nuts
Wednesday	Two-ingredient banana pancakes	Baked beans with ground lean beef	Pimiento cheese-stuffed mini bell peppers	Crispy egg noodles with tofu & peanut sauce	Dark chocolate frozen banana bites
Thursday	Breakfast beans with microwave-poached egg	Balsamic pork tenderloin	Radishes with green goddess dressing	Seitan bbq sandwiches	Blueberry gratin
Friday	Southwestern waffles	Sesame-garlic beef & broccoli with whole-wheat noodles	Baked parsnip chips	Zucchini-chickpea veggie burgers with tahini-ranch sauce	Buckwheat crepes
Saturday	Pistachio & peach toast	Lamb chops with mint pan sauce	Baked zucchini waffle fries with creamy herb dip	Lemon-pepper linguine with squash	Caramelized pineapple with raspberries
Sunday	Sweet potato kale breakfast salad	Chicken kebabs	Chili-lime brussels sprout chips	Mushroom shawarma with yogurt-tahini sauce	Raspberry banana sorbet

Week 06

Days	Breakfast	Lunch	Snack	Dinner	Dessert
Monday	Egg tartine	Grilled mahi-mahi	Grilled chicken and cherry salad	Grain bowl with chickpeas & cauliflower	Chia pudding
Tuesday	Cannellini bean & herbed ricotta toast	Red pepper & parmesan tilapia	Fresh taco salad	Roasted vegetable bowls with pesto	Dark chocolate and cherry brownies
Wednesday	Creamy blueberry-pecan oatmeal	Chimichurri baked flounder	Shrimp and rice noodle salad	Stuffed sweet potato with hummus dressing	Avocado brownies
Thursday	Everything bagel avocado toast	Grilled halibut with blueberry salsa	Indian garbanzo bean salad with pitas	Veggie & hummus sandwich	Banana mousse
Friday	Banana chocolate chip mini muffins	Walnut and oat-crusted salmon	Maple mahi-mahi salad	Roasted vegetable & black bean tacos	Chocolate bark with espresso and toasted nuts
Saturday	Two-ingredient banana pancakes	Grilled blackened shrimp tacos	Stone fruit salad with baked goat cheese coins	Mushroom & tofu stir-fry	Dark chocolate frozen banana bites
Sunday	Breakfast beans with microwave-poached egg	Green curry salmon with green beans	Wilted spinach salad with pears and cranberries	Roasted root veggies & greens over spiced lentils	Blueberry gratin

Week 07

Days	Breakfast	Lunch	Snack	Dinner	Dessert
Monday	Southwestern waffles	Chicken, brussels sprouts & mushrooms one-pot pasta	Homemade multi-seed crackers	Honey glazed salmon	Banana mousse
Tuesday	Pistachio & peach toast	Honey-roasted chicken thighs with sweet potato wedges	Mini bell pepper pebre	Bean burger	Chocolate bark with espresso and toasted nuts
Wednesday	Sweet potato kale breakfast salad	Slow-cooked ranch chicken and vegetables	Pimiento cheese-stuffed mini bell peppers	Grilled shrimp	Dark chocolate frozen banana bites
Thursday	Egg tartine	Skillet lemon chicken & potatoes with kale	Radishes with green goddess dressing	Chicken kebabs	Blueberry gratin
Friday	Cannellini bean & herbed ricotta toast	Garlic cashew chicken casserole	Baked parsnip chips	Pan-seared steak with crispy herbs & escarole	Buckwheat crepes
Saturday	Creamy blueberry-pecan oatmeal	Roast chicken & sweet potatoes	Baked zucchini waffle fries with creamy herb dip	Mushroom & tofu stir-fry	Caramelized pineapple with raspberries
Sunday	Everything bagel avocado toast	Beef stir-fry with baby bok choy & ginger	Chili-lime brussels sprout chips	Easy pea & spinach carbonara	Raspberry banana sorbet

Week 08

Days	Breakfast	Lunch	Snack	Dinner	Dessert
Monday	Banana chocolate chip mini muffins	Healthy baked halibut	Grilled chicken and cherry salad	Grilled salmon with cilantro-ginger sauce	Chia pudding
Tuesday	Two-ingredient banana pancakes	Steamed tilapia in wine sauce	Fresh taco salad	One-pot garlicky shrimp & spinach	Dark chocolate and cherry brownies
Wednesday	Breakfast beans with microwave-poached egg	Miso-maple salmon	Shrimp and rice noodle salad	Farfalle with mushrooms and spinach	Avocado brownies
Thursday	Egg tartine	Charred shrimp & pesto buddha bowls	Indian garbanzo bean salad with pitas	Thai chicken risotto	Banana mousse
Friday	Cannellini bean & herbed ricotta toast	Roasted salmon with sautéed balsamic spinach	Maple mahi-mahi salad	Roasted sweet potatoes with chili and seeds	Chocolate bark with espresso and toasted nuts
Saturday	Creamy blueberry-pecan oatmeal	Crumb-coated red snapper	Stone fruit salad with baked goat cheese coins	Prawn and spinach angel hair pasta with prawn oil	Dark chocolate frozen banana bites
Sunday	Everything bagel avocado toast	Halibut soft tacos	Wilted spinach salad with pears and cranberries	Beef spaghetti	Blueberry gratin

Frequently Asked Questions

Is it essential to completely eliminate fats from the diet to maintain heart health?

No, it is not necessary to completely avoid fats on your heart healthy diet. Although it's essential to limit the intake of unhealthy saturated as well as trans fats, it is also equally important to consume healthy fats in moderation.

Are all carbohydrates harmful to health?

No, not all carbohydrates are dangerous to your health. It is imperative to differentiate between refined carbohydrates and complex carbs. Refined carbohydrates, found in ingredients like white bread, sugary cereals, and pastries, can have a negative impact on heart health. However, complex carbs have been linked to a lower risk of heart disease.

Can I have eggs on a heart-healthy diet?

Certainly, you can use eggs as a part of a heart-healthy diet. While eggs were once thought to contribute to high cholesterol levels, recent studies show that the effect of such cholesterol on blood cholesterol levels is limited for most individuals.

Are artificial sweeteners a better option than sugar for heart health?

These can be a useful alternative to sugar for people with diabetes or those looking to reduce calorie intake. They do not raise blood sugar levels and can help with weight management. However, the long-term effects of artificial sweeteners on heart health are still being studied. It's important to use them in moderation and focus on whole, unprocessed foods as the foundation of a heart-healthy diet.

Is a vegetarian or vegan diet heart-healthy?

Yes, a carefully planned vegetarian or vegan diet can be a great option for a heart health. Plant-based diets provide rich sources of fiber, vitamins, minerals, and antioxidants while naturally low in cholesterol and saturated fat. However, it's important to maintain a balanced intake of essential nutrients like iron, vitamin B12, and omega-3 fatty acids. While on this diet you should consume adequate plant-based protein sources, like legumes, tofu, tempeh, and quinoa, on this diet.

Conclusion

By completing this cookbook, you have made a big move towards prioritizing your heart health. However, it's imperative to remember that adopting a heart-healthy diet is not a one-time thing but a lifelong commitment. I would like to encourage you to put into practice the information, 150 recipes, the 8 weeks-meal plans, and practical tips you have found throughout this cookbook. Try to experiment with new ingredients and flavors. Remember, every little step counts, whether it's replacing the unhealthy ingredients with healthier ones, making mindful decisions at the grocery store, or engaging in physical activity. Your heart will thank you for the time and effort you put in. So, go ahead and try the recipes, explore the meal plans, and make this heart-healthy diet an integral part of your daily life.

******

Note from the Author:

Hello, Health Hero!

You've aced another recipe, and we're thrilled you're with us. But before you go, know this: your words matter.

Two Birds, One Stone

We're indie authors on a budget; your review means a lot to us and keeps us going. Plus, it lights the way for others fighting heart issues. It's a win-win!

Time's Ticking—Speak Up!

The faster you review, the quicker we help more people. Heart health waits for no one.

Thanks a lot for staying with me!

Grace Garner

Conversion Tables

Weight conversion tables

Ounces (oz)	Grams (g)	Tablespoons (tbsp)	Teaspoons (tsp)
0.5	14.2	1	3
1	28.4	2	6
1.5	42.5	3	9
2	56.7	4	12
2.5	70.9	5	15
3	85.0	6	18
3.5	99.2	7	21
4	113.4	8	24
4.5	127.6	9	27
5	141.7	10	30

Pounds (lbs.)	Ounces (oz)	Grams (g)
1	16	453.6
2	32	907.2
3	48	1360.8
4	64	1814.4
5	80	2268.0

Liquid Conversion Table

Measurement	Metric	US Customary	Imperial
Teaspoon (tsp)	5 ml	1/6 fl oz	1/6 fl oz
Tablespoon (tbsp)	15 ml	½ fl oz	½ fl oz
Fluid Ounce (fl oz)	30 ml	1 fl oz	1.04 fl oz
Cup (c)	240 ml	8 fl oz	9.61 fl oz
Pint (pt)	473 ml	16 fl oz	19.22 fl oz
Quart (qt)	946 ml	32 fl oz	38.43 fl oz
Liter (l)	1000 ml	33.814 fl oz	35.195 fl oz
Gallon (gal)	3.785 l	128 fl oz	153.72 fl oz

Temperature Conversion Table

Fahrenheit	Celsius (approximate)
300 °F	150 °C
325 °F	160 °C
350 °F	175 °C
375 °F	190 °C
400 °F	200 °C
425 °F	220 °C
450 °F	235 °C
475 °F	250 °C

References

Appel, L. J., Sacks, F. M., Carey, V. J., Obarzanek, E., Swain, J. F., Miller, E. R., . & Laranjo, N. M. (2006). Effects of protein, monounsaturated fat, and carbohydrate intake on blood pressure and serum lipids: results of the OmniHeart randomized trial. JAMA, 294(19), 2455-2464.

Benjamin, E. J., Virani, S. S., Callaway, C. W., Chamberlain, A. M., Chang, A. R., Cheng, S., . & Khan, S. S. (2019). Heart disease and stroke statistics—2019 update: a report from the American Heart Association. Circulation, 139(10), e56-e528.

Dinu, M., Pagliai, G., & Sofi, F. (2018). Mediterranean diet and multiple health outcomes: an umbrella review of meta-analyses of observational studies and randomized trials. European Journal of clinical nutrition, 72(1), 30-43.

Estruch, R., Ros, E., Salas-Salvadó, J., Covas, M. I., Corella, D., Arós, F., . & Fiol, M. (2013). Primary prevention of cardiovascular disease with a Mediterranean diet. New England Journal of Medicine, 368(14), 1279-1290.

Estruch, R., Ros, E., Salas-Salvadó, J., Covas, M. I., Corella, D., Arós, F., . & Serra-Majem, L. (2013). Primary prevention of cardiovascular disease with a Mediterranean diet. New England Journal of Medicine, 368(14), 1279-1290.

Estruch, R., Ros, E., Salas-Salvadó, J., Covas, M. I., Corella, D., Arós, F., . & Lamuela-Raventos, R. M. (2013). Primary prevention of cardiovascular disease with a Mediterranean diet supplemented with extra-virgin olive oil or nuts. New England Journal of Medicine, 368(14), 1279-1290.

Kodama, S., Saito, K., Tanaka, S., Maki, M., Yachi, Y., Asumi, M., . & Sone, H. (2009). Cardiorespiratory fitness as a quantitative predictor of all-cause mortality and cardiovascular events in healthy men and women: a meta-analysis. JAMA, 301(19), 2024-2035.

Mente, A., de Koning, L., Shannon, H. S., & Anand, S. S. (2016). A systematic review of the evidence supporting a causal link between dietary factors and coronary heart disease. Archives of Internal Medicine, 169(7), 659-669.

Mozaffarian, D., & Rimm, E. B. (2006). Fish intake, contaminants, and human health: evaluating the risks and the benefits. JAMA, 296(15), 1885-1899.

Roth, G. A., Mensah, G. A., Johnson, C. O., Addolorato, G., Ammirati, E., Baddour, L. M., . & Garcia-Garcia, H. M. (2020). Global burden of cardiovascular diseases and risk factors, 1990–2019: update from the GBD 2019 study. Journal of the American College of Cardiology, 76(25), 2982-3021.

Sacks, F. M., Svetkey, L. P., Vollmer, W. M., Appel, L. J., Bray, G. A., Harsha, D., . & Karanja, N. (2001). Effects on blood pressure of reduced dietary sodium and the Dietary Approaches to Stop Hypertension (DASH) diet. New England Journal

Satija, A., Bhupathiraju, S. N., Rimm, E. B., Spiegelman, D., Chiuve, S. E., Borgi, L., . & Hu, F. B. (2017). Plant-based dietary patterns and incidence of type 2 diabetes in US men and women: results from three prospective cohort studies. PLoS Medicine, 14(7), e1002039.

Te Morenga, L. A., Howatson, A. J., Jones, R. M., & Mann, J. (2014). Dietary sugars and cardiometabolic risk: systematic review and meta-analyses of randomized controlled trials of the effects on blood pressure and lipids. American Journal of Clinical Nutrition, 100(1), 65-79.

Warburton, D. E., Nicol, C. W., & Bredin, S. S. (2006). Health benefits of physical activity: the evidence. Canadian Medical Association Journal, 174(6), 801-809.

Yang, Q., Zhang, Z., Gregg, E. W., Flanders, W. D., Merritt, R., & Hu, F. B. (2014). Added sugar intake and cardiovascular diseases mortality among US adults. JAMA Internal Medicine, 174(4), 516-524.

Made in the USA
Las Vegas, NV
22 November 2023

81234769R00059